OTHER TITLES OF INTEREST FROM ST. LUCIE PRESS

Organizational Transformation and Process Reengineering

Evolution of Management Theory: Past, Present, Future

Seven Fatal Management Sins: Managerial Malpractice (A Wake-Up Call)

Macrologistics Management

Creating Productive Organizations

The New Leader: Bringing Creativity and Innovation to the Workplace

The Motivating Team Leader

Real Dream Teams: Seven Practices Used by World-Class Team Leaders to Achieve Extraordinary Results

Leadership by Encouragement

Reengineering the Training Function: How to Align Training with the New Corporate Agenda

How to Reengineer Your Performance Management Process

Sustaining High Performance: The Strategic Transformation to a Customer-Focused Learning Organization

For more information about these titles call, fax or write:

St. Lucie Press
100 E. Linton Blvd., Suite 403B
Delray Beach, FL 33483
TEL (407) 274-9906 • FAX (407) 274-9927

$S{}^t_L$

PROBLEM SOLVING
for
RESULTS

PROBLEM SOLVING for RESULTS

William Roth
James Ryder
Frank Voehl

S_L^t

St. Lucie Press
Delray Beach, Florida

Printed and bound in the U.S.A. Printed on acid-free paper.
10 9 8 7 6 5 4 3 2 1

ISBN 1-57444-018-7

Phone: (407) 274-9906
Fax: (407) 274-9927

$S{}^t_L$

Published by
St. Lucie Press
100 E. Linton Blvd., Suite 403B
Delray Beach, FL 33483

DEDICATION

To Eric Trist

My teacher and friend.
One of the founders of the systems approach
to management theory.
A man who remains to me
an ongoing model for
completeness and humility. With thanks.

William Roth

To my mother, Jane S. Harrison, and father, James A. Ryder, Sr.

Whose love, high standards, understanding,
and confidence have provided me with
a life-long inspiration to succeed and
the ability to stay the course
in the face of life's challenges.

James A. Ryder, Jr.

To Jerry Lippman

Who never met a problem he couldn't solve and

To Jay Spechler

Who taught me how to put it all together.
Thank you for being my friends.

Frank Voehl

TABLE OF

CONTENTS

PREFACE

Problem solving has been going on since the beginning of time. It is traditionally one of the major chores in all facets of our lives. As the centuries have passed, the art of problem solving has necessarily evolved. It has evolved because the problems we must deal with have become increasingly sophisticated. The number of variables involved has grown. The range of potential solutions has expanded. The web or "mess" of interrelated problems to which ours belongs and which affect ours has spread.

Today, in the world of work, due to the increasing level of competition, the cost of incorrect solutions is rapidly growing. More effective problem solving, therefore, is critical to success. As a result, society has turned problem solving into a science complete with schools of thought on how best to shape the workplace culture so that it will encourage effective efforts, on how best to shape vehicles to facilitate these efforts, on what the best problem-solving tools and techniques are, and, finally, on how best to fit the critical pieces of problem-solving efforts together.

Problem Solving for Results was written as a study of these pieces—culture, vehicles, tools, and techniques—and as an exploration of their relationships. The book was written from a systems perspective.

In Chapter 1, we begin by addressing the issue of workplace *culture*. We focus initially on the development of a reward system that will facilitate effective problem solving. We do so because we believe that an organization's reward system does more to shape its culture than anything else. We use Abraham Maslow's *hierarchy of needs* as a frame of reference for our argument.

Chapter 2 begins by introducing four different *attitudes* toward problem solving—reactive, inactive, hyperactive, and preactive—all of which treat problems as a threat. It then defines an alternative, the interactive attitude, which helps turn problems into opportunities as well.

Next, the chapter addresses *perspective,* which helps shape both culture and attitude. It identifies the origins and characteristics of the systems perspective and talks about how this perspective facilitates problem solving. Finally, Chapter 2 identifies three problem-solving vehicles— task forces, quality teams, and autonomous work groups. It discusses the strengths and weaknesses of each and how they can be combined.

Chapter 3 gets down to the nitty-gritty and looks at the *techniques and tools* available for problem-solving efforts. The chapter identifies four broad categories—individual, group, systemic, and productivity measuring—into which all techniques and tools can be fit. It spells out in detail the steps in 40 of them and then identifies situations where each can be used effectively and how they can be combined.

Chapter 4 talks about *approach,* about how to start organization change efforts so that they can generate the necessary culture, maintain the right attitude, build the most appropriate vehicle, and properly utilize the right tools and techniques. It addresses the issue of training and discusses whether it should be introduced up front or on the job and how training in problem-solving efforts should be organized. It gives an example of how the necessary training was effectively introduced in one corporation.

In Chapter 5, Frank Voehl introduces one of the models available for systemic problem-solving efforts, the *Quality Journey Problem-Solving Process.* He spells this model out, step by step, for readers.

Finally, Chapter 6 presents a comprehensive case study involving an electronics firm that both sells and services equipment. The major problem addressed is the lack of necessary information flowing between management and employees and between company and customers. The case study explores in depth the trials and tribulations of attempting to change the culture of an organization by attempting to introduce the Quality Journey Problem-Solving Process and the necessary teams, techniques, and tools.

The major obstruction in this case study, as in most, is the differing perspectives of various employees. Jim Ryder shows us, in great detail, his version of what can be done to deal with these differences and what can be done to draw employees together into a comprehensive, successful problem-solving effort.

The contribution of Danny Finch, owner of Media Dynamics (a design firm specializing in graphic design and interactive multimedia production, located in North Palm Beach, Florida), was invaluable in preparing the illustrations that appear in the case study.

Problem solving is not a new topic. Many books have been written on it. Few, however, have "hit the mark." This is because they have lacked the necessary focus and the full range of necessary ingredients.

Success in problem-solving efforts is the result of appropriate resources being mustered and appropriate process skills being applied. While the reader/problem solver must obviously provide the resources, *Problem Solving for Results* offers a comprehensive framework for the required perspective and process skills, along with a simplified problem-solving model and an integrated case study which helps bring it all to life.

Good reading.

William Roth
James A. Ryder, Jr.
Frank Voehl

AUTHORS

William Roth is currently a full professor at Allentown College St. Francis de Sales in the Lehigh Valley of Pennsylvania. He has previously published four quality-related books, the most recent being *The Evolution of Management Theory: Past, Present, Future* with St. Lucie Press. He has also published a large number of articles in leading journals.

Dr. Roth earned his Ph.D. from the Wharton School in management sciences. He has consulted in quality, organization design, and strategic planning for some twenty years. Recently he took the lead in designing a comprehensive quality training program called "Beyond TQM: The Systems Approach to Quality Improvement," sponsored by the AQP and being offered nationwide through a network of colleges and universities. He is a member of the ASQC Education Division Strategic Planning Committee.

James A. Ryder, Jr. is currently the managing principal of The Jim Ryder Group, a management consultant firm specializing in performance and quality improvement. Clients include firms in financial services, healthcare, and manufacturing.

Previously, Mr. Ryder spent four years at Qualtec Quality Services as a quality improvement consultant, assisting various organizations as a trainer, facilitator, and consultant. Much of his early experience in quality improvement was obtained at Florida Power & Light during the time when FPL successfully challenged for the Deming Prize.

Prior to FPL, Mr. Ryder operated a retail electronics business, which provided insight into customer satisfaction, manufacturing practices, and human services. Earlier in his career, he practiced corporate law at Ryder System, Inc.

Mr. Ryder holds a B.S. in business administration from the University of North Carolina at Chapel Hill, a J.D. from the University of Florida, and an M.B.A. from the University of Miami. He is presently a member of the ASQC and the Association for Quality and Participation.

Frank Voehl has had a 20-year career in quality management, productivity improvement, and related fields. He has written more than 200 articles, papers, and books on the subject of quality and has consulted on quality and productivity issues, as well as measurement system implementation, for hundreds of companies (many Fortune 500 corporations). As general manager of FPL Qualtec, he was influential in the FPL Deming Prize process, which led to the formation of the Malcolm Baldrige Award, as well as the National Quality Award in the Bahamas. He is a member of Strategic Planning committees with the ASQC and AQP and has assisted the IRS in quality planning as a member of the Commissioner's Advisory Group.

An industrial engineering graduate from St. John's University in New York City, Mr. Voehl has been a visiting professor and lecturer at NYU and the University of Miami, where he helped establish the framework for the Quality Institute. He is currently president and CEO of Strategy Associates, Inc. and a visiting professor at Florida International University.

On the local level, Mr. Voehl served for ten years as vice chairman of the Margate/Broward County Advisory Committee for the Handicapped. In 1983, he was awarded the Partners in Productivity award for his efforts to streamline and improve the Utilities Forced Relocation Process, which saved the state of Florida some $200 million over a seven-year period.

CREATING THE RIGHT CULTURE

THE CHALLENGE

The world of business is becoming increasingly turbulent. Change is occurring moreso at a geometric (1,2,4,16) than at an arithmetic (1,2,3,4) rate. It has been estimated, for example, that more new technology has appeared in the last 20 years than in the rest of human history combined. At the same time, the level of competition is rising rapidly as strong new players enter the arena. Partnerships of different kinds are springing up between companies offering the same product, between companies offering complementary products, between companies on different continents, and between companies with very different cultures.

At least partially as a result of these advances in technology and our rapidly expanding perspective, facets of operations which were once relatively straightforward are growing more complex. Management systems are in a state of crisis. The top-down, hierarchical, "make no decisions without my okay," channeled mode of operation no longer suffices. The need for ever-increasing speed and accuracy is forcing us to flatten chains of command and to break down the walls between functions.

One of the traditional management responsibilities being most strongly challenged is problem solving. Increasingly we are hearing calls to push problem-solving and decision-making authority downward, to encourage the solution of problems on the lowest possible level. The days of Frederick

Taylor's Scientific Management are gone—when emphasis was on simplifying jobs to the point where lower level employees did not have to think, when human potential was ignored and employees were conditioned to function like simple, mindless machines that do what they are told rather than trying to contribute.

Managers are no longer equipped to make or capable of making the growing number and variety of necessary decisions themselves. Employees must begin to think more for themselves and take corrective action, instead of simply complaining to or seeking a solution from management.

In addition to the growing complexity of operations, a second key factor reinforcing this trend is changes in the workplace itself. Technology has made traditional, centralized, office-based operations somewhat obsolete. Yet modern-day employees continue to travel long distances in order to meet the same job responsibilities they could perform just as well or better at home or at a local "mini-office" complex outfitted with appropriate equipment. This does not make sense in terms of time, expense, efficiency, or the environment.

Despite our realization that change is inevitable and will be beneficial, we, as a culture, are having difficulty moving away from an outdated mindset. We continue to operate "the way we've always done it" because that is the arrangement our traditional management system, which centers on control rather than facilitation, has spawned. It is another product of Frederick Taylor's Scientific Management and the endless search for the most efficient means of monitoring employee activities. This reactive rather than interactive approach to an increasingly complex issue is causing our quality of life, both at home and in the workplace, to suffer.

Eventually, of course, things will, indeed, change. It is inevitable. The most instinctual desire beyond survival which has driven civilization historically has been the desire to improve the quality of life for both individuals and for society as a whole. From this perspective, we have done well in terms of achieving our objectives and have come a long way in a relatively short period of time.

Our present difficulty in accepting advantageous change, therefore, is not new. Rather, it is normal. It is a coping mechanism to protect us from the unknown. It is reflected in individuals with power trying to hang onto the status quo because they are comfortable with it and not secure enough to accept change, no matter how obvious the need and benefits. It is another one of the stumbling blocks that have littered the pathway of progress but which will eventually be swept away by the irresistible forces of social evolution, like all the others before it.

When this happens, the workplace, management systems, and problem solving will become increasingly decentralized. The nature of work itself will change radically and we will, hopefully, begin as a culture to remember its development-related purpose.

A large-scale education effort is one of the support systems we must organize if we are to make the desired transition as smooth as possible. Two things will be key if such an education effort is to be effective. The first is that top-level management must be helped to rethink its concepts of organizational attitude and organizational design. The second is that employees on all levels must concentrate on improving their problem-solving skills.

In terms of the top-level management rethinking exercise, those involved must be willing to look beyond what has brought success in the past and shift into the new world paradigm. They must move beyond the need for an organizational structure carved in stone with rigid lines of communication and authority. They must become more flexible and willing to risk creative new arrangements. They must become more pragmatic and be willing to go with what works in terms of problem solving. They must honestly and openly address the following issues:

1. Which employees should be responsible for addressing which problems?

2. Who should have access to what information in order to address problems effectively?

3. In what format and when should problems be solved?

4. What is the best way to integrate the results of individual and group efforts?

5. What is the best way to make sure that such a participative approach is effective in terms of the long-term objectives of the organization?

These are among the issues that will be addressed in this book. This is no easy challenge. These are tough issues that affect every facet of an operation. They cannot be addressed in the most effective manner until the necessary changes in organizational culture have occurred.

THE RIGHT REWARD SYSTEM

Perhaps the toughest of the challenges we are talking about, and the most threatening of the necessary changes, will involve the reward system. It must be reshaped. The reward system is the cornerstone of all operations. More than any other system, it determines the culture of the organization and frequently its structure and processes. It affects such things as the way employees on all levels interact with each other and with employees on other levels, the size of departments, the willingness of employees to take risks, and the way information is guarded or shared.

As long as reward systems continue to pit managers against each other and continue to create an adversarial relationship between management and the work force, the shift toward the cooperative atmosphere necessary for more effective problem solving will not occur. Each group will continue to sub-optimize in favor of its own self-interest, to the detriment of the system as a whole.

Employees are not altruistic. The major priority during their work lives is not to satisfy customers (in-house or external), bosses, or owners. Rather, the major priority is to shape a job in that way which will best satisfy their own needs and desires.

Unless the company also enjoys success, of course, such satisfaction will not occur. Customers, bosses, and owners (or "stakeholders" as systems professionals call them) are indeed important, but the most important stakeholder (in the eyes of the individual employee) is the individual employee himself or herself. That is as it should be in any pragmatic society. That is the realization upon which the free enterprise system was built.

Most of the models upon which the current quality improvement movement depends, for example, make the customer the most important target. This has happened because our quantitatively oriented business community favors measurement and numbers. Customer satisfaction is one of the factors that we are set up to measure in an improvement process.

We also make the customer the most important target because focusing on improving customer relations is much more fruitful in terms of public relations and marketing.

We have confused the ends with the means, the results with the producers. Customer satisfaction is a result produced by committed employees. The focus, therefore, in organization improvement efforts should be to get employees effectively involved and do what is necessary to develop the necessary level of commitment.

This can be accomplished by incorporating satisfaction of employee needs into the model. But to which employee needs and desires should we be paying attention? Which ones are important? Which ones are the company's responsibility? If everyone wants to drive a new company-provided car, should we feel obliged to satisfy that desire? Must we, in essence, be willing to "give away the store"?

The evidence refutes such fears. In poorly run organizations, where management is out to get the most from employees for the least, the employees will indeed take the company for everything they can. In companies like this, such fears are realistic. They are, however, also largely the result of management's attitude.

On the other hand, in organizations that show true concern and respect for employees, such standoffs do not usually occur. Workers want to be and understand that they are part of a team. They are willing to make sacrifices of time, effort, and even money if such sacrifices are necessary to the survival and healthy growth of the organization, as long as everyone else, from top to bottom, has the same attitude.

When the team and the organization do well, the employees want to enjoy the victory along with their mates and be rewarded fairly for their contribution.

BEGINNING WITH THE BASICS

What employees define as their needs, in a respectful atmosphere, is reasonable and, in fact, differs little from what they define as their needs in private life. The nature of basic human needs has been questioned throughout the history of mankind, and the answer has changed little over the centuries. Psychologist Abraham Maslow described the range of these needs thoroughly in the middle of this century (Maslow, 1954). His definition, which incorporates the work of many others, seems complete, has not been greatly improved upon, and can be related back to the workplace with relative ease.

Physiological Needs

On his first foundational level, Maslow places physiological needs (those necessary to physical survival). These include food, water, shelter, and an environment capable of sustaining life. These needs are obviously the most basic. When one of the requisite inputs is missing, the penalty for not replenishing it is death. The quest for it may often supersede that for all others.

In the workplace, physiological needs can be framed in terms of salary, i.e., earning enough money to be able to afford the necessary food, liquids, and environmental needs. As people stopped growing their own food and building their own homes and began to work for others who headed companies that manufactured goods to be sold in sometimes distant marketplaces, salary became the primary focus.

Although it spurred the growth of wealth, the resulting scenario frequently led to disaster. For example, during the early Industrial Revolution in England, it was estimated that an average weekly factory wage allowed the purchase of only three days of food for a family of four. Today, many single working mothers in low-level jobs do not earn enough to adequately satisfy the physiological needs of their families and must depend upon public assistance to do so.

In the modern-day workplace, therefore, despite seemingly tremendous wealth, adequate salary remains the major issue for most. People must earn enough money before they can even consider addressing the other needs in Maslow's hierarchy. If the source of adequate income disappears, emphasis must revert immediately to it, no matter how far up the hierarchy we have progressed.

Safety Needs

Safety needs are on Maslow's second level. They include security, protection from physical injury, freedom from fear, and so on.

Security at home frequently depends upon security at work. In today's workplace, job security has become a major and very controversial topic.

Some firms identify job security as their number one priority. They promise employees they will do everything possible to ensure it. According to their way of thinking, job security is a critical ingredient of long-term improvement of the bottom line. On the other hand, some firms boldly declare that no one's job is secure. The company's major responsibility is to earn money for its owners. The company, therefore, does whatever is necessary to improve the bottom line.

The latter group has defined downsizing as a valuable tactic to quickly produce numbers that "look good." In reality, however, it wreaks havoc with employee morale as well as productivity (which is tied to employee morale), although a number of apologists would loudly dispute this statement.

Quite simply and in line with Maslow's reasoning, people do not work as well for and are loath to commit to employers or projects once it is made clear that the bosses feel no allegiance to the employees, no matter how good their performance might be, and see them as expendable.

In addition, temporary workers (or "temps") are becoming increasingly popular as a way to cut costs. Their pay scale can be kept relatively low, no benefits are currently required, and temps can be dismissed relatively easily.

The following scenario is becoming increasingly familiar. First, a company downsizes in order to cut costs, which batters the morale of both survivors and those released. Then, management realizes that the company is chronically understaffed and brings in temps as an alternative to rehiring. This deals another blow to the permanent work force, as people wonder who will be replaced next. The temps, who understand the climate and know what their real role is, do not feel very secure either. Top management, on the other hand, which is far removed from the pain, frustration, and fear and which is unaware of or unconcerned about Maslow's hierarchy, is pleased because the bottom line looks good, at least for the short term.

Despite a growing number of articles protesting the practice of downsizing, its use seems to be accelerating, particularly in the United States. While the skill and education levels of employees are steadily increasing, management's respect for employees seems to be decreasing.

Competitors in Japan and Europe apparently have a better feel for the reality of the situation. They are included in the category of those who downsize, but only as a last resort. In Japan, in fact, when things do not go well, it is the executives and managers who take the blame and penalize themselves by cutting their own salaries. Sometimes they even bow out rather than penalize the workers who have faithfully followed their lead. It would be a disgrace to do otherwise.

Physical safety, the second consideration in this category, is another major on-the-job concern of employees on all levels. Nobody wants to get hurt. When accidents do happen, individual focus in terms of the hierarchy is frequently forced back to the basic survival/physiological need level. In terms of workplace safety, the United States is doing pretty well, partially because companies have come to realize that injured workers can cost them a great deal and partially because of government regulation.

Belongingness

Maslow's third level, after physical survival (pay) and security/safety needs have been satisfied, has to do with belongingness. The need for belongingness, which begins in infancy, is well documented in the scientific literature. Children who feel rejected by parents and other key figures in their lives never really recover. They might learn to cope with the emotions involved so that they can function almost normally, but the scars remain.

The need for belongingness persists throughout our school years, during which we form peer groups. It also persists into our working lives, where we frequently get as much done while socializing over coffee, in the cafeteria, or on the phone as we do at our desks.

Some companies realize this and encourage an open, trusting atmosphere. A whole class of consultants spends time conducting exercises to open channels, improve communication, and take the mistrust out of relationships between departments. T-groups and wilderness challenges are two of the techniques currently used.

Another movement in the right direction is the quality improvement movement. A comprehensive quality effort centers on employees forming teams in order to work together to make improvements in products, manufacturing processes, management systems, and the work environment itself. Effective team building is based on trust, empowerment, and respect, which are also keys to generating a sense of belonging.

Esteem

Maslow's next level covers the need for esteem. People need to feel that they are making a contribution which they themselves can respect. In most cases, such self-respect results from the impression one's contribution makes on others—family, friends, peers, co-workers, bosses. Society understands this need. It works to build esteem in the young through school programs, scouting programs, teams, and clubs which work to ensure that everyone who tries is a winner and is rewarded.

Things tend to become murkier when we enter the world of work, where the traditional reward system is highly competitive and focuses on individual achievement. Because of this often competitive/conflictive atmosphere, the ploy is frequently to promote one's own accomplishments while denigrating those of others, which fosters envy and suspicion instead of respect.

In this type of atmosphere, employees obviously are less willing to share their ideas. Doing so puts them at risk. The result of joint exercises, therefore, is rarely respect and the desired end product—self-esteem.

Self-Actualization

On the highest level of Maslow's hierarchy is the need for self-actualization. This involves the individual's desire to gain the opportunity and inputs necessary to realize his or her positive potential as a human being to the fullest possible extent. The desire for self-actualization is the driving force behind societal evolution.

In the workplace, self-actualization may seem impossible for most employees. Jobs frequently involve hours of dull, repetitive, nondevelopmental work performed in order to earn the input/money which, hopefully, will allow the employees to do what they want during nonworking hours.

Unfortunately, the number of nonworking hours available for such developmental activities appears to be decreasing. While it increased steadily from the middle of the Industrial Revolution through the 1950s, in the United States at least, the weekly number of working hours the average family currently spend on the job just to maintain a suitable standard of life is growing again.

There are, however, several bright spots. One is that the number of jobs that are developmentally challenging is increasing. Teaching is an example. Education is rapidly becoming a life-long process for most of us, and the number of teachers will have to increase. The teaching process will also change by becoming more innovative and creative. Technology will become a major tool, making our classes richer and more interesting.

Research and consulting are also growing fields that are becoming more challenging. Some believe that a majority of jobs will eventually be held by consultants rather than traditional full-time employees. More efficient technology will replace humans in factory and clerical jobs, which will free employees to move about more easily, to focus on improvement-related projects, and to incorporate education and research into their activities.

It is also believed that an increasing number of people will begin to shift back and forth between industrial and teaching jobs on a regular basis, combining the challenges of a "real-world" sector with those of the education sector and providing more developmental opportunities.

HOW DO WE GET THERE?

We are not getting what we want as employees in the workplace. What is stopping us in almost every case can be traced back at least partially to a reward system which is antithetical to the necessary changes, which breeds disrespect and distrust, which makes tight controls over employee activities necessary, which by its very nature is contradictory to a team approach, and which discourages the open sharing of information, ideas, and opinions.

The traditional reward system has actually never been very efficient in terms of guiding and encouraging the positive expenditure of employee energy. Too much "negative energy" has been wasted defending oneself or neutralizing possible threats. The problem has been that we have had nothing to compare it to.

But now that is changing. Other players in the world market are introducing reward systems which improve productivity and profitability in ways that only the most gridlocked management corps can ignore. Quite simply, instead of conflict and win–lose competition, they are encouraging cooperation and a win–win atmosphere.

At the same time, a growing amount of research on the subject shows that a majority of employees would prefer an arrangement which reinforces the team approach; open sharing of information, ideas, and opinions; etc.

The reward system of the future is becoming increasingly well defined. It is a system that encourages the highest level of commitment in all employees and encourages them to use their full range of potential most effectively to increase productivity.

Such a system will obviously include certain well-defined characteristics. First, everyone's take will necessarily be tied to the bottom line in such a way that it will increase in good years and decrease in bad. The most frequently cited example of the bottom-line-based salary system is Lincoln Electric, where 50 percent or more of everyone's yearly reward can come as part of their bonus package, which is tied directly to the overall success of the company. Lincoln Electric has consistently been one of the most successful companies in the United States. No one quits and no one is laid off. Everyone feels they belong and everyone feels they contribute.

Second, everybody will know what everybody else earns. This will eliminate game playing and deception. It will also help bring salaries into line.

Third, a team approach to rewards will be used, preferably at multiple levels—department, division, and organization. Emphasis on individual performance will decrease. Emphasis on contribution to team efforts will increase. This should reduce the amount of negative energy expended and the amount of politicking that goes on.

If such a system is instituted properly, it should eliminate the supposed need for performance evaluations. It should also shift the emphasis from outperforming co-workers to encouraging the fullest possible realization of each other's work-related potential.

This may sound simple, and it is. It has been proven to work in a growing number of companies.

In terms of Maslow's hierarchy of needs, starting at the first level with physiological needs, the pay scale under such a system would obviously become more reasonable, and employees would be more likely to look out for each other's interests.

In terms of Maslow's second-level safety needs, decisions that affect job security would no longer result from the whim of a CEO or the votes of a few top-level executives. They would, instead, be understood and accepted before the fact by the work force, and the various alternatives would be explored participatively

The team approach upon which such a reward system is based would obviously enhance feelings of belongingness, Maslow's third-level need. The contributions of team members would be applauded because they would now benefit everyone, thus also enhancing self-esteem, Maslow's fourth-level need.

Finally, all of this would help satisfy the need for self-actualization, which lies at the fifth and highest level of Maslow's hierarchy.

ONWARD AND UPWARD

In summary, organizational problem solving as a means to produce the best results must be a participative activity. When it is, the richness of the contribution made by employees will depend upon their level of commitment to the cause. People naturally want to commit to the organizations for which they work. It adds purpose to their lives.

As mentioned, people are not altruistic. They need to know that they will benefit in some acceptable way for their efforts. The benefits they seek from work have to be spelled out. The reward system must offer the benefits, but it must tie them to the success of problem-solving efforts in order to encourage both commitment and effectiveness. This is the ideal situation, and it is certainly not out of reach. It is just different, and anything different, no matter how obviously superior, takes some getting used to.

We hope that by nudging the culture in the right direction, by improving our approach to problem solving, and by gradually introducing a more cooperative and profitable atmosphere, we will encourage top-level management to eventually address the issue of rewards.

What kind of organization-wide attitude toward problem solving will be most useful? How should we alter organizational perspective and structures to most effectively take advantage of employee expertise in terms of the activities involved? These are some of the issues that are addressed in the next chapter.

SHAPING THE RIGHT ATTITUDE, PERSPECTIVE, AND VEHICLE

THE RIGHT ATTITUDE FOR CHANGE

Problem solving is the essence of any business operation. It is also the most interesting part of such operations. New businesses must deal with problems concerning funding, location, advertising, suppliers, licenses, taxes, technology, record keeping, competition, insurance, transportation, staffing, and organization. Ongoing businesses must solve a constantly expanding array of problems generated by social and technical forces which daily grow more numerous and complex. They must also deal with the problem of defining the organization's future, a problem which is never completely solved.

One factor that strongly affects an organization's success in this area is its attitude toward problem solving. Several different ways of reacting to problem-solving situations have evolved.

The most unrealistic, but by no means least popular, is to simply ignore them. Russell Ackoff, who along with Peter Drucker and W. Edwards Deming is considered one of the trinity of modern-day management theory, calls this the *inactive* attitude or approach to planning/problem solving in his book *Redesigning the Future.*

Organizations that have gridlocked themselves with boundary building and turf-protection stratagems tend to adopt this attitude. Nobody wants to take a chance.

Top-level management in such organizations, however, while putting itself in position to take the lead in all problem-solving efforts, does not always have the time or the range of expertise necessary to do so effectively. As a result, many solutions never materialize, many are slow in coming in an effort to avoid making a mistake, and too often, those that do eventually arrive are not well thought out.

The inactive attitude is frequently found in companies where the reward system pits employees against each other. The problem-solving skills of most employees in such organizations, due to lack of usage, are limited. As the environment and markets become more turbulent and competitive, the chance of such companies surviving decreases rapidly.

A second planning attitude that can be related to problem solving has been labeled by Ackoff as *reactive*. The objective of companies practicing reactive problem solving is to limit the number of problems employees have to deal with by establishing rules for every possible situation. This attitude is frequently found in hierarchical organizations with firmly entrenched bureaucracies. Workers are not encouraged to think. Their chief responsibility is to learn the rules and to follow them.

The frantic rate of change experienced in the modern-day environment makes this approach extremely time consuming and often futile. Many such rules are obsolete before they have been written. This happenstance approach causes confusion, creates an atmosphere of confrontation, and ultimately, perhaps, increases the severity of those problems which do eventually surface, working their way through the closely knit fabric of control.

Organizations with a reactive attitude cling to tried-and-true ways of doing things and are suspicious of innovation and creativity, no matter how great the apparent need. To their leaders, new approaches are not worth risking. The problem-solving skills possessed by employees in such companies are usually well learned and proven, but limited to a dangerous degree. Organizations with a reactive attitude, however, strongly believes that such skills are sufficient. Because all the acceptable solutions have already been worked out, problem-solving sessions are mainly spent defining the most appropriate match, with upper-level management (because of its greater experience and in order to ensure that control is maintained) again functioning as the final judge.

Organizations that practice reactive problem solving tend to be old and large and to have a traditional reward system. The all-encompassing maze of rules has evolved, at least partially, as an attempt to limit the infighting such a reward system fosters by providing a final authority.

A third problem-solving attitude (added with tongue in cheek) is *hyperactive*. This attitude calls for quick, aggressive attention to problems which always seem to be in a crisis stage—call a meeting, form a task force, concentrate employee expertise on attempts to find an immediate and usually short-term answer, and then return to business as usual until the next crisis arises or is generated.

This attitude usually results from the management style of an extremely ambitious, aggressive boss who wants to be in the spotlight and enjoys the feeling of power that such situations bring. A lot of the problems which quickly turn into crises are actually created by such bosses. They also, of course, make the final decision based in large part on their own frequently hidden agenda. Loyal employees are expected to agree and implement solutions delivered by their leaders without question.

Hyperactive problem-solving efforts are totally orchestrated, so that the skill level of everyone but the boss is unimportant. Employees just need to know how to appear to be intensely involved, how to nod their heads emphatically, and how to make periodic, short, innocuous, supportive comments.

The next attitude identified by Ackoff which can be applied to problem solving is *preactive*. A majority of organizations at least aspire to this one. It is very much in vogue. Preactive problem solvers try to predict problems they will have to face in the future and prepare solutions in advance. They do this to get a jump on both the problem and their competition. Forecasting and a range of problem-solving techniques, many of which are discussed in this book, are used. Consultants and internal experts are relied upon heavily to contribute to the process.

The preactive attitude considers employee input important, but feels that it should be carefully monitored and channeled. Employees are told what to work on. Once they have outlined alternatives within the carefully defined parameters of their project, the alternatives are presented to a boss, who is responsible for the final decision.

Preactive problem solving occurs in companies which still sport traditional reward systems, have not yet questioned them, but are beginning to realize the value of and need for employee input and commitment and are looking for ways to encourage it. Many of them are altering their organizational design with this goal in mind. By so doing, they have taken the first step along the pathway to comprehensive change.

INTERACTIVE IS THE FUTURE

One thing the four attitudes thus far discussed—inactive, reactive, hyperactive, and preactive—have in common is that they treat the problem as an interloper, a factor alien to the operation, one which should be ignored, restricted as thoroughly as possible, confronted forcefully once it has successfully penetrated organization defenses, or prepared for in advance. In any case, problems are treated as the enemy.

A fifth attitude, the interactive attitude, takes a different perspective. It views problems as having a positive as well as negative side. It views them as opportunities as well as obstructions. With this in mind, the fifth attitude defines problem solving as an integral, ongoing part of any healthy operation rather than a nuisance at best and a waste of time and resources or a serious obstacle at worst. It defines problem solving as a pastime critical to positive organization and individual development.

Interactive problem solving stems from the growing realization that organizations are capable of designing their own futures in order to avoid problems, rather than waiting for them to occur and reacting or even trying to predict them.

For organizations to successfully cultivate this attitude in terms of problem solving, they must have a clear vision of their purpose which is accepted by all employees. They must also have a clear understanding of the role each of the functions and individuals within the organization must play in terms of that purpose. Such organizations must be capable of learning constantly from their environment and adapting.

It is no longer the company that comes up with the best one-shot solution that wins; rather, it is the company that is able to keep its vision in tune with an increasingly turbulent environment and is able to constantly readjust flexible structure and processes in order to avoid falling behind.

Such a scenario, of course, calls for radical changes which will affect every facet of an operation. To succeed, three basic organizational characteristics must evolve:

1. All employees must be encouraged to identify problems and work on their solutions. Participation must be present in the broadest sense of the term.

2. The interactive attitude and resultant activities must become part of the culture, a key part of daily operational activities.

3. These interactive activities must span the entire organization, extend into the environment, and be well integrated.

Interactive problem solving is the future. At this point in time, however, not many companies are practicing it. Though "interactive" has become a buzzword in good currency, "talking the talk," in this case, is much easier than "walking the talk." Our traditional workplace culture precludes at least two of the three necessary organizational characteristics defined above.

The first pitfall has to do with participation. Allowing employees to truly participate takes a great deal of trust. Most managers, even if they want to, are unwilling to trust their reports to the necessary degree for a range of reasons, including pressure from above, their training, and fear of losing control.

The second pitfall is that developing a well-integrated, comprehensive network of problem-solving activities requires breaking down walls, ceasing internal competition, and overcoming suspicion between functions. In most cases, this will not happen until we rethink our reward system.

What we currently have in the workplace, then, instead of an approach to problem solving, is an aggregate of competing opinions from which decision makers are forced to choose. These opinions, of course, usually result from the perspective of their source.

For example, in a business situation, a young employee operating a machine or filing records might say that the repetitious, unchallenging nature of the job is the problem underlying a relatively low productivity level which is not rising. The employee's older foreman or office manager might say that the problem is that young people today no longer take pride in their work. The director of personnel might see the problem as one of improper staffing patterns. The company president might decide that the problem is due at least partially to the fact that employees have been kept in jobs which can be done more efficiently by technology. Finally, a consultant called in might offer the opinion that the problem results from a lack of proper training for managers.

Which opinion is correct in this situation? Which defines the real problem? Should they all be considered correct? Do they all actually define parts of the same problem?

If this last possibility proves true, how can such a many-headed hydra be attacked and dealt with effectively? In most cases, while the various opinions might be listened to, management's decision will be of the "either–or" type. Management will first try its luck with the "either" solution, but will find that it does not really solve the problem. Then management will drop the "either" solution entirely and will switch to the "or" solution, but the "or" solution will, of course, generate results that are not much better.

THE RIGHT PERSPECTIVE FOR CHANGE

What is the real issue, then? What underlies all this confusion and the inability of organizations to put together a system capable of dealing interactively with problems? The real issue keeping us from achieving a good, long-term solution in this situation and many like it is, as we have said, perspective, which shapes attitude and is, therefore, critical to culture. The key to understanding this conclusion, however, is the realization that what we are talking about is management's macro rather than its micro perspective.

What does that mean? Quite simply, it means that we, as a business culture, continue to think analytically when the time has come to start thinking synthetically as well. Again, what does that mean? In order to explain, we have to go back into history, several hundred years to be exact. Since the Renaissance and the beginnings of what we call "modern science," the emphasis has been on analysis. "Analysis" means that scientists have broken down the object or event under investigation in an attempt to identify all its component parts. Once the parts have been identified, the investigator has carefully studied them. The belief has been that by thoroughly understanding the nature of the parts of the system, scientists could understand the nature of the system itself.

This approach was critical to the development of the physical sciences. For some disciplines, it was, in fact, the only feasible alternative. For example, because of the limitations of early technology and theory, astronomers were incapable of formulating an accurate overview of the system being explored. They had to piece this vision together from a very limited series of observations delineating often random bits of the puzzle.

In terms of the workplace, this approach has been most useful with strictly mechanical systems. The wheel and axle, the lever, and the inclined plane have been identified as the basic design elements of all machines. Different combinations of these basic elements have made different manufacturing processes possible. Modifications of each element plus the design of more elaborate combinations have made a greater variety of increasingly sophisticated mechanical systems available.

In view of the above, all one has traditionally needed in order to understand such a system has been a definition of the elements involved, an explanation of modifications to these elements, and an explanation of how the elements involved have been combined.

The moment, however, that the human operator became a factor in the formula, problems arose. Initially, attempts were made to define the operator as just another mechanical part of the system. Such a role facilitated evaluation of the employee's performance through analysis—identify the employee's various needs and then formulate ways to manipulate these needs in order to make the human "machine" more productive.

Many started from this perspective (e.g., Frederick Taylor searched for the "one best way." Frank Gilbreth introduced the concept of motion studies, Henry Gantt developed the Gantt chart, and Harrington Emerson emphasized standardization), and many managers and consultants still do.

With social (human) systems, however, it was eventually found that this approach did not work as well as with purely technical systems. Social systems were much more complex, and the "parts" involved (especially when emotions came into play) were constantly changing. Also, human participants, it turned out, did not especially appreciate being treated like machine parts and reacted accordingly.

Another reason this approach could not work, as scientists eventually realized, was that all systems, and especially social systems, are more than simply the sum of their parts. In terms of social systems, any sports fan, for example, knows that a team is more than an aggregate of individual players. The team has a tradition, a style of play, an attitude, and fans, all of which contribute to its performance.

A third reason the analytic approach did not work as well with social systems and the social side of sociotechnical systems was that they are part of a larger system or environment which cannot successfully be ignored. The larger system helps shape the behavior of the embedded system. In order to fully understand the embedded system, therefore, we must also understand the containing system. In order to unravel the operation and interaction of a floor full of junior executives, we must take into consideration the pressures exerted by their bosses.

This need is becoming increasingly obvious for technical systems as well. As they become more powerful and consume growing quantities of our natural resources, the role of technical systems in the containing environment is being scrutinized more intently. For example, environmental issues are of increasing importance in decisions concerning the way we as a nation generate, distribute, and consume energy.

This new, more holistic way of looking at organizations was labeled, not surprisingly, the "systems" approach. A system is a set of interrelated parts that work together to reach a common goal, objective, or ideal which has either been defined for the parts by others (as with machine parts) or has been defined by the parts themselves (as with any team). Three types of systems exist in the workplace—social systems, technical systems, and sociotechnical systems.

A *social* system is a set of two or more individuals who interact. Any work force or segment of a work force with a common purpose is a social system. An entire factory or office staff is a social system. Assembly-line workers, computer operators, salespeople, secretaries, internal consultants, middle managers, boards of directors, and janitorial staffs are all more specifically defined social subsystems which together comprise the larger system.

Each individual worker belongs to more than one social system in an organization. An employee can be part of a social subsystem of assembly-line workers or secretaries responsible to a foreman or to an office manager. At the same time, this employee can be part of a team responsible to an executive for achieving certain production quotas and quality standards. Finally, the employee can be part of an organization responsible to customers and investors.

A *technical* system is a set of two or more techniques and/or tools that interact to produce a certain quantity and quality of goods and services. "Techniques" include the expertise (usually gained through training) necessary for the production of a certain item, whether material (shoes) or nonmaterial (information). "Tools" are implements used to facilitate techniques—a cobbler uses knives and needles to shape and sew together shoes much as a junior executive uses a computer to generate reports.

A *sociotechnical* system is a set of one or more individuals and one or more techniques/tools interacting to produce a certain quantity and quality of goods or services that facilitate achievement of a goal, objective, or ideal defined by the individuals who control that system, sometimes with the help of techniques and/or tools.

Social, technical, and sociotechnical systems are always embedded in a larger system. For example, the sociotechnical system that puts together left front doors in an automobile assembly plant is contained by a larger sociotechnical system that assembles car bodies. This sociotechnical system, in turn, is part of a system that produces entire automobiles which, in turn, is part of a company that manufactures and distributes them. The company system, in turn, is part of a society which uses automobiles for transportation, and so on.

The systems approach, as noted, shifts the emphasis from understanding the parts as thoroughly as possible to understanding the relationships *between* these parts on all levels and understanding the system-wide dynamics created by these relationships. Then, as West Churchman says in *The Systems Approach* (1968, p. 11), it leads to identification of "the most effective organization of your system (its parts, relationships and system-wide dynamics) in terms of fulfilling its role in (the) containing system."

The systems approach obviously necessitates movement away from analysis and toward synthesis. Instead of always looking inward and breaking things down, systems thinkers begin looking moreso at the whole and examining a relationship in terms of that whole and in terms of the larger whole of which it is a part.

To further clarify the distinction between the traditional analytical approach and the systems approach, suppose two consultants were called into a company to address the same problem—bad labor–management relations. The analytical consultant would focus immediately on the "pieces" by spending as much time as possible with as many individual employees on both sides of the issue in order to solicit their views. He or she would try to discover who the troublemakers were and to work with, train, or get rid of them so that the remaining "pieces" might fit better.

The systems consultant, in contrast, would focus on the glue that holds the pieces together—the communication process, access to information, the reward process, the training process, the evaluation process, the punishment process, etc. According to this consultant, bad relations result mainly from weaknesses in the way these processes were set up. His or her approach would be to get the process right, and a majority of the personal problems and bad attitudes will correct themselves.

This shift from an inward to an outward orientation broadens our perspective tremendously. During the long reign of the analytical approach, emphasis was focused on "what" and "how." We asked *what* the system was supposed to achieve in terms of short-term goals and *how* the pieces of the system should be organized in order to achieve those goals in the most efficient manner. We asked *what* models of sailboats or televisions or hairbrushes the company should gear up to produce in order to maximize sales and *how* bonus systems should be organized so that individual salespeople could achieve or surpass their sales quotas.

The synthetic approach with its outward perspective encourages us to address the question of "why" as well. We are beginning to ask *why* something is being produced and consumed in terms of the needs and desires of all those individuals and social systems that affect or are affected by the processes involved. We are wondering, for example, whether the current boom in computer technology is, in the long run, going to be totally advantageous to society or whether, in fact, one end result might be a great deal of suffering and social turmoil.

We have realized that our joint sociotechnical systems, in both the private and work sectors, have become so powerful and so interdependent that even a minor shift in emphasis or a minor miscalculation in one can set off a far-reaching chain reaction of repercussions. As a result of this new awareness, the "why" question has become a must.

THE RIGHT VEHICLE FOR CHANGE

What does an organization look like when it has adapted an interactive attitude toward problem solving, has begun thinking systemically, and has decided that synthesis and the "why" question are just as important as analysis and the "what" and "how" questions? What is its structure, and what are its processes in terms of problem solving? Which is the major activity of its social system now that technology is handling most of the grunt work?

Let's start with structure. As mentioned, interactive problem solving is, by definition, participative, ongoing, organization-wide, and integrated. This means that everyone who is going to be affected by solutions must, in some way, be encouraged to contribute on an ongoing basis. It does not mean conducting a survey to gather a total cross-section of opinions and then discussing each opinion individually whenever an issue arises. Rather, it means that a vehicle must be put in place which allows representatives of stakeholder groups to examine, question, and contribute to tentative solutions generated by a sponsoring group or team.

What should the vehicle look like? There are several alternatives. We will start with the least sophisticated. The most familiar version to working people is the task force, a hand-picked group of employees, usually including both middle managers and hourly employees, who work on a specific problem defined and assigned by upper-level management. Participants come up with either a set of alternative solutions or one solution which they consider the best and present it to upper management, which makes the final decision. The task force then disbands.

Integration often does not exist between the efforts of different task forces. They can pop up and disappear all over an organization at the whim of managers. They are popular in the competition/conflict-driven workplaces with an inactive, reactive, hyperactive, or preactive attitude because management stays in charge—assigning the problem to be addressed, participating in and often leading the exercise, and making the final decision.

Task forces also appear in organizations with an interactive attitude, but their role is different. In order to make the most effective use of employee expertise at all levels, interactive organizations build their problem-solving approach around one of two vehicles. The first and less sophisticated of these is the improvement team network. This network is the core piece of successful quality efforts. It is composed, initially at least, of separate hourly and management teams that span the organization. The teams in the network represent all functions and meet regularly, usually on a weekly or bi-weekly basis.

Quality improvement teams identify their own projects. Their efforts, however, are closely integrated by a web of facilitators trained by a head facilitator who reports directly to the organization or unit leader. In order to maintain the necessary momentum and control, all quality teams must obey a set of ground rules agreed to by all participants at the beginning of the process.

One key ground rule is that team members have access to anyone in the organization for required information or decisions. Another is that when such a request is made, the responder has a limited period of time in which to respond. If a response in not forthcoming, the head facilitator, and then the organization leader, is called upon to encourage it.

A third critical ground rule is that anyone who will be affected by a proposed solution must have knowledge of it and a chance to contribute before the team begins implementation. Obviously, any change in products, manufacturing processes, management systems, or the work environment designed by an hourly team will affect the manager. The manager, therefore, eventually becomes a player and can have decisive input, because all final decisions are reached through consensus (Roth, 1991).

The differences between this and the task force approach are considerable. First, interactive problem-solving teams, both hourly and management, are truly empowered. They are allowed by management to pick their own projects and to define their own solutions without the guidance of superiors. This gives real ownership and shows a greater level of respect. The key is that team members invite the manager to participate when his or her input is eventually needed, rather than the process being aimed and led by a manager from the start.

Task forces are created in this scenario when a problem is addressed which spans several functions or several teams, usually at the hourly level because management teams are frequently cross-functional. Task forces can also be created by top-level management around projects it considers important that are not being addressed. The difference is that when the assigned problem is adequately dealt with, the task force disbands, while quality teams in the network remain in place and begin working on another item from their list.

The two vehicles, improvement teams and task forces, can exist side by side and complement each other in an interactive environment. They cannot, however, always co-exist in a preactive environment due to the fact that the level of empowerment proposed for team members would not be acceptable.

The team approach can and has been mounted in organizations with traditional reward systems. If it succeeds and the company's profits increase as a result, one of the teams will eventually make the design of a fairer and more realistic reward system one of its projects. Such an initiative has been known to spell the rapid demise of team efforts. It has also, however, been known to trigger a successful transition to the new cooperative mentality we are all ultimately seeking.

The second and most sophisticated vehicle that organizations with an interactive attitude build their problem-solving efforts around is the autonomous work group. Employees included in such groups do everything team members do, but continuously and on the job rather than in weekly or biweekly meetings.

In some cases where a team approach has survived and thrived long enough for the ground rules to be absorbed into the corporate psyche, the teams stop meeting formally and their work is absorbed into the daily production unit process so that autonomous work groups or something similar to them evolves.

Interactive organizations that use autonomous work groups divide their operation into functions. They then give a managerless team of workers control over each function. Members of this group are responsible for producing an agreed upon number of items, be it cabinets, car doors, ads, sales, formulas, etc. They decide how to do so. They decide which group member will complete which task and when to rotate tasks. They do the job skills training and pick new group members when someone leaves. Managers take on the role of a facilitator rather than a decision maker. They provide resources and expertise to the groups only upon request.

All members of autonomous work groups are paid the same. This is obviously different from the improvement team network setup. While the latter eventually evolves toward the point where a more equitable reward system is designed, autonomous work groups start with such a system in place.

Task forces can again exist side by side with autonomous work groups and complement them.

ONCE AGAIN, WHO'S IN CHARGE?

In interactive organizations, all participants are allowed, by the ground rules, to define problems they consider important. This does not mean that a team or work group will chose to work on one individual's idea, at least at first. It does mean, however, that the idea will, at some point, receive attention.

A second process issue that middle managers in particular want to address when they form teams is who, exactly, is responsible for what decisions concerning what problems. In inactive, reactive, hyperactive, and often preactive organizations, again, no one is quite sure. At the same time, for a variety of reasons, people are afraid to ask. As a result, things tend to be pushed upward.

This might be good for the self-esteem of top-level managers, but it is not very effective in terms of time, the quality of solutions, and generating employee commitment.

In truly interactive organizations, as we have said, decision-making authority is pushed downward to the lowest possible level, instead of upward. While managers, as stakeholders, provide input, employees do not turn to them automatically for all the answers. Emphasis is on involving those who will be affected the most by the solutions.

After problem identification and solution come the definition of action steps and implementation. In organizations with the first four attitudes, once a solution is agreed upon it is placed on management's desk, where it might sit forever, be changed arbitrarily, or be implemented piecemeal. Management oversees and shapes implementation.

In an interactive organization, implementation is the responsibility of the sponsoring team or work group. The logic behind this shift is simple. The employees who lead the effort to generate the solution understand it best. It is their idea. Therefore, they will be more persistent in terms of getting it right. Also, because there are more team members than there are top-level managers, things will happen faster.

For the same reasons, teams and work groups in interactive organizations are also responsible for monitoring results of the improvement effort and fine tuning, when necessary.

Example

A secretaries' team was formed as part of a quality-improvement process instituted recently by the Allentown, Pennsylvania city government. Members were not satisfied with the in-house phone directory. It had been reorganized by consultants two years before, but was difficult to use. Some of the headings were misleading, there was no answer at some of the phone numbers listed, some of the numbers listed were incorrect, and callers were often transferred several times before reaching the party they were calling.

The secretaries took on the project of reorganizing the directory. They started from scratch. Representatives from each department listed the information their people could provide and the numbers to call. The team then broke the book down into simple, well-defined categories. Finally, they developed a quick access list of the most frequently used numbers for each department and printed it on a separate sheet to be placed next to each phone.

The secretaries developed a draft of their revised listing and distributed it for a test run. Only two months later, team members, with feedback from all departments, fine-tuned the directory and printed it.

THE NEXT STEP

Now that we have defined the attitude, the types of vehicles, and the general process characteristics which best facilitate problem solving, it is time to move on to the problem-solving activity itself. Do we just turn team and work group members loose and let them do their own thing? Do we say, "Hey, you're picking your own problems. Now you figure out how to address them." Or do we train participants?

If we decide that training is a good idea, what do we teach our employees? There are many problem-solving techniques floating around and being sold. How do we decide which one to use or which will produce the most effective results in our specific situation? How do we even gain an accurate overview of what is available?

These are some of the questions that will be addressed in the next chapter.

PICKING THE RIGHT TECHNIQUES AND TOOLS

Problem-solving techniques/tools can be divided into four categories:

1. Those used to improve the creativity and/or to enhance the problem identification and problem-solving skills of the individual

2. General techniques used to improve the creativity and/or to enhance the problem identification and problem-solving ability of groups

3. Systems-oriented techniques used to work with problem networks or "messes" (as systems scientists call them)

4. Tools used specifically to measure productivity

In this chapter, we shall identify a comprehensive cross-section of techniques/tools in all four categories, describe how they work, and judge their effectiveness.

TECHNIQUES/TOOLS FOR INDIVIDUALS

All of the techniques/tools discussed here can be utilized by individuals in a group as well as by solitary problem solvers. Emphasis, however, is on overcoming self-imposed, individual constraints.

Most of the techniques/tools described have to do with the manipulation of something. Human thought processes tend to fall into habitual patterns. A specific type of stimulus brings a specific type of response. By changing the way a problem or potential solution is formulated, we can sometimes break out of our self-imposed ruts and develop a new perspective. By reorienting our thought patterns or adding new ones, we can modify our vision of reality, sometimes in useful ways.

To help accomplish the above objective, the tools/techniques presented in this section are divided into four subcategories: word games, attribute manipulation, elaborations, and analogy making. Examples of each are provided.

Individual Techniques Based Upon Word Games

Word Manipulation

This category includes several techniques that focus on the manipulation of both the way words are put together and the words themselves in order to give sentences or phrases new meaning. They can be introduced in at least two ways:

1. State the problem or potential solution verbally or symbolically, and then reorganize the words or symbols in the statement to suggest different approaches or alternative solutions. For example, the problem statement

    "Assembly-line workers don't listen to their supervisors."

    can be changed to read

    "Supervisors don't listen to assembly-line workers."

    This transition leads problem solvers to explore more carefully the attitudes and motivations of the supervisors making the accusation.

2. Substitute similar or more specific words for those in a problem or potential solution statement. In the preceding example, the statement could be altered to read

> "Assembly-line workers don't respect their supervisors."

or

> "Assembly-line workers often can't hear what their supervisors are saying above the noise."

The first modification offers a reason for their not listening. The second suggests the nature of potential solutions.

Lateral Thinking

In his book entitled *Lateral Thinking*, Edward DeBono discusses the need to challenge all verbal assumptions, recurring themes, clichés, and recurring obstacles. Perhaps his most sophisticated offering is an exercise that encourages practitioners to relate to the problem a number of concepts developed through free association, hopefully inspiring new insights.

The issue at hand might be inadequate employee input into the planning process. The first step in the lateral thinking technique is to randomly name an object, animal, or color, picking any alternative that comes to mind. Let's use "dog" as an example. The second step is to list down the left side of a sheet of paper as many attributes and concepts that can be thought of which are related to "dog." The last step is to transform each characteristic or concept into a problem-solving approach.

A dog might be characteristically "friendly." An approach to solving the problem of inadequate employee input which takes this characteristic into consideration might be for those running the process to improve relationships with all participants. A dog might also be considered to be a "protector." The related approach would be to ensure the right of all stakeholders to contribute to the problem-solving process without harassment or fear of retribution.

Forced Connections

Forced connections is a technique similar to lateral thinking and is used mainly to address technical system problems. For example, in attempting to define a new transportation system, we might ask what the result would be if the attributes of a car were joined to those of a train. Answers might include "a car that can go anywhere roads exist without being driven" or "a train that does not need track."

This technique can also be used to address social system problems. For example, the problem might be a bad relationship between the sales force and the investment department of an insurance firm. The question addressed might be: "What would happen if the attributes of the two units were combined?" Answers would help identify areas where the units complement each other, as well as areas where they conflict. The questioner might also discover possible compromises, as well as syntheses that would strengthen both operations.

Individual Techniques/Tools Based Upon Attribute Manipulation

Previously defined attributes of a problem or potential solution can be organized in order to suggest alternative approaches. This can be done by matching, combining, grouping, ordering, elaborating upon, dissecting, challenging, viewing from another perspective, and so on.

Matrix

One traditional means of identifying alternatives is cross-classification. A matrix is a tool used to facilitate the cross-classification process. It helps define the results of forced relationships between problem or potential solution attributes which have been divided into two or three categories. A matrix is designed to ensure that every possible combination is identified. The tool was developed originally to help solve technical problems. It can, however, also be used to deal with problems found in social systems.

Sliding Column Method

Another cross-matching technique is S.J. Parnes' sliding column method. When using this technique, individuals again categorize and list desired or required solution attributes.

If the problem is employees complaining about the hours they work, the categories of potential solution attributes might include working hours, overtime policy, or self-scheduling. The categorized lists are then laid side by side and shifted up and down to allow different fits. The variety of combinations created by this shifting should suggest alternatives. For example:

Working Hours	*Overtime Policy*	*Self-Scheduling*
Shorter	Employee choice	Weekend work
Fixed shifts	Cut down on	Work at home

One fit might be shorter working hours/cut down on overtime/work at home, and a second fit might be fixed shifts/employee choice/weekend work.

Definition of Grouping Similarities

Practitioners of this technique list attributes of problems or potential solutions, group the ones that seem similar, and then try to define what makes those assigned to each group similar to one another and different from the attributes assigned to other groups. This helps them to better understand the true nature of the problem. It also helps them to better define the relationship between the various attributes.

Solution Preference Identification

Practitioners of this technique list potential solutions in order of preference and then try to identify what their preferences are based on. This technique helps problem solvers better define the nature of the desired final solution.

Morphological Analysis

Morphological analysis, developed by Dr. F. Zwicky, is an expanded version of the sliding column method. The process begins with the practitioner thinking of as many attributes of potential solutions as possible and listing them. Once the list is complete, the attributes are combined in every way possible. The final step is to design solutions around every individual grouping of attributes.

For example, if the problem is lack of an appropriate incentive system for managers, the four potential solution attributes listed might be more money, more free time, educational opportunities, and promotions. Possible combinations of these four potential solution attributes include:

1. More free time to moonlight and make more money

2. Financing for job-related and/or nonjob-related education

3. Promotions that include raises

4. Free time to take courses

5. Promotion to a position that allows more free time

6. The promise of a promotion if certain educational goals are achieved

7. Free time to take advantage of educational opportunities paid for by the firm

8. A promotion and salary increase if certain educational goals are achieved

9. A promotion that offers more free time and a salary increase

10. Free time to take advantage of education opportunities which can lead to a promotion

The intent is that one of these groupings will produce an acceptable novel solution.

Morphological Forced Connection

Morphological forced connection, a modification of morphological analysis, was presented by Don Koberg and Jim Bagnall. In this technique, the attributes possessed by potential solutions are defined, but instead of immediately combining the results, practitioners list as many alternatives as they can think of beneath each attribute. For example, if the attributes are more money, more free time, educational opportunities, and promotions, the alternative lists might read:

More Money	*Educational Opportunities*
Stock options	Night courses at school
Bonuses	Day course in-house
Profit sharing	Self-study programs

Promotions	*More Free Time*
Opportunity for lateral movement	Longer weekends
Opportunity to develop new operations and grow with them	Longer lunches
Opportunity to develop a dual advancement track	Longer vacations

Practitioners then combine alternatives from the different lists to define novel problem solutions.

Refer to the case study presented in Chapter 6 for an example of how a team found this process useful in resolving an early dilemma in Step 1 of its Quality Journey.

Techniques Based Upon Elaboration

This subcategory includes various checklists. A checklist is a list of possible conceptual manipulations that are in some way relevant to the problem being addressed.

Osborne Checklist

Alex Osborne offers perhaps the best-known general-purpose checklist. Manipulations suggested in his offering relate to both technical and social systems. They include:

Put to other uses? New ways to use it? Other uses if modified?

Adapt? What else is like this? What other ideas does this suggest? Does it offer parallels? What could I copy? Whom could I emulate?

Modify? New twists? Change meaning, color, motion, odor, form, shape, etc.?

Magnify? What to add? More time? Greater frequency? Stronger? Larger? Thicker? Extra value? Additional ingredient? Exaggerate? Multiply?

Minify? What to substitute? Smaller? Condensed? Miniature? Omit? Streamline? Split up? Understate?

Substitute? Who else instead? What else instead? Other ingredient? Other material? Other process? Other power? Other place? Other approach? Other tone of voice?

Rearrange? Interchange components? Other pattern? Other layout? Other sequence? Transpose cause and effect? Change pace? Change schedule?

Reverse? Transpose positive and negative? How about opposites? Turn it backward? Turn it upside down? Reverse roles? Change shoes? Turn tables? Turn the other cheek?

Combine? How about a blend, an alloy, an assortment, an ensemble? Combine units? Combine purposes? Combine appeals? Combine ideas?

Manipulative Verbs Technique

The checklist developed by Koberg and Bagnall is composed of what they call manipulative verbs. Many of the suggested actions are more exotic than those called for by Osborne. They include:

Multiply	Dissect	Soften	Stretch
Divide	Distort	Fluff-up	Extrude
Eliminate	Rotate	By-pass	Repel
Subdue	Flatten	Add	Protect
Invert	Squeeze	Subtract	Segregate
Separate	Complement	Lighten	Integrate
Transpose	Submerge	Repeat	Symbolize
Unify	Freeze	Thicken	Abstract

Interaction Associates Checklist

The checklist developed by Interaction Associates is extensive. It includes 67 idea manipulations or "strategies." Each is accompanied by a description of powers and limitations and by an exercise which shows how the strategy can most effectively be used. The list includes the following actions:

Build up	Select	Exemplify	Symbolize
Eliminate	Plan	Compare	Simulate
Work forward	Predict	Relate	Test
Work backward	Assume	Commit	Play
Associate	Question	Defer	Manipulate
Classify	Interpret	Leap in	Copy
Generalize	Adapt	Hold back	Systemize
Focus	Reduce	Combine	Record
Release	Exaggerate	Separate	Retrieve
Force	Understate	Change	Search
Relax	Incubate	Vary	Hypothesize
Dream	Display	Cycle	Guess
Imagine	Organize	Repeat	Define
Purge	List	Verbalize	Transform
Transform	Check	Visualize	Substitute
Translate	Diagram	Memorize	Randomize
Expand	Chart	Recall	

Expert Consultant

Another elaborative technique is the expert consultant technique. As a means of developing a different perspective, exercise participants think of a person they know and respect who might approach the problem they are attempting to solve differently because of different personality characteristics and/or experiences. They then "become" that person and attempt to address the problem as they think he or she would, developing the ideas and approaches they think he or she might use.

Problems-Within-Problems

The next offering is a pair of elaborative problem-solving techniques which encourage reorientation. The problems-within-problems approach dissects the problem network addressed in an attempt to discover the subproblems of which the network is composed. The goal is that an understanding of these subproblems will help practitioners better define the original problem network and suggest possible solutions.

Seek-the-Larger-Network

The seek-the-larger-network alternative is the opposite of the problems-within-problems technique. This technique attempts to define the larger network of which the immediate problem is a part. Suppose that the immediate problem is that a department lacks access to all the information required to do its job properly. Instead of attacking this problem directly, you would investigate the degree to which the entire division enjoys access to information. What you learn at the higher level might change your perspective concerning the local situation. It probably will also suggest a more elaborate set of solution steps.

If possible, it is advantageous to combine the problems-within-problems and seek-the-larger-network techniques in order to simultaneously look both inward and outward during the exercise. This, of course, is the systems approach and allows the participants to develop the most holistic definition of the problem network.

Ask Why Five Times

One final technique which helps an employee reach and define the real problem, instead of simply attacking symptoms, is the ask why five times technique, used by Taichi Ohno at Toyota. Suppose the original problem is that the department secretary is not transferring incoming calls to salespeople in a department quickly enough. Instead of telling her to start doing her job or else, ask "why." When you find out that she is away from her desk a lot, ask "why" again. When you find out that she is delivering messages personally because intradepartment phone lines are continuously busy or salespeople are away from their desks, ask "why" again. When you find out that the phone system has no voice mail feature, ask "why" again. When you find out that management planned to purchase such a service but has not yet done so, ask "why" again. Obviously, there can be more than five "whys" involved in this exercise.

Individual Techniques Based Upon Analogy Making

All analogies are based on the inference that if two or more things agree in some respect(s), they will probably agree in others.

Relationship Analogies

Problem solvers using the relationship analogies technique list analogies that define the relationship of key elements in a problem situation. If the problem is management–labor relations, a worker might say that he has experienced a "slave to master," "victim to mugger," or "dictator to subject" relationship. His manager, on the other hand, might say that he has been party to a "parent to youngster," "teacher to pupil," or "truant officer to delinquent" relationship.

Once listed, these descriptions can be discussed with others to decide which or what combination is most accurate. The next step would be to develop a list of analogies to describe what the relationship ought to be ideally.

Attribute Analogy System

The attribute analogy system was developed by Koberg and Bagnall. After identifying the critical attributes possessed by an object, technical system, social system, or sociotechnical system, instead of listing alternatives beneath each one as in morphological forced connections, participants list analogies. For example, if the problem is to improve efficiency in the word-processing department, key attribute categories could be workload, skills involved, experience level, and incentive system. The workload might be heavy but sporadic. An analogy would be "compressed to waste time" or "hurry up and wait."

Ideas resulting from these analogies might include hiring more personnel to work shorter hours, using temps, rescheduling input to even out the work flow, and developing additional duties for personnel in the department.

Synectics

The last technique presented here is William Gordon's synectics. It seems that no two reviews explain this technique in the same way. There are two possible explanations for this. One is that the technique is too complex for anyone but the founder to understand. The second is that Gordon purposely incorporated this vagueness in order to enhance the technique's flexibility.

Synectics uses analogies, metaphors, and similes to define relationships between things. Four approaches are possible. The first is to develop "direct analogies." The purpose is to discover how the problem network being discussed is similar to other things. Suppose the problem is a rapidly growing market of which a young company wants to take advantage. An analogy might be a hive of bees that has just discovered a bathtub full of honey. What similarities might exist in the reactions of the two organizations?

The second approach, the development of "personal analogies," involves a type of role-playing. The person(s) using this approach must become the company, as a physical entity or a body. As the company, the person must gather certain things from his or her environment in order to grow. He or she must also provide certain goods and services. How does a person best utilize his or her body parts in order to accomplish this objective?

The third approach, called "compressed conflict," involves identifying the essence of the problem as a functional description of the desired outcome in which conflicts or paradoxes are condensed. This essence is then formulated as an analogical question which generally captures the uniqueness of the situation. After the question has been formulated, a metaphor is sought to address it.

Ackoff and Vergara use an example in "Creativity in Problem Solving and Planning" that includes two people in the same room. One wants to read in a quiet setting while the other wants to listen to loud music. An analogical question which captures the uniqueness of the situation is: "How can a loud silence be produced?" An appropriate metaphor might be: "A bullet that embeds itself in one body cannot strike another." The metaphor suggests that the music lover use headphones.

The last approach described is the "fantastic analogy." Users must allow their imaginations to ramble unrestrained, to concoct the most bizarre solutions possible. Suppose you are a young organization faced with the enviable task of having to meet the demands of a rapidly growing market. You must pretend that you are a wizard capable of producing any type of organization you desire with a snap of your fingers. What would you produce to meet this challenge? What would the organization's attributes be?

Synectics has been used mainly in group settings. It is included here because its emphasis is on releasing the power of the individual mind and imagination, rather than deriving the most from group interaction.

Evaluation of Techniques Used to Enhance Individual Problem-Solving Ability

Now let's evaluate the problem-solving techniques for individuals in terms of strengths and weaknesses. Each technique, for example, is designed to encourage boldness and originality. At the same time, none fully utilizes the intelligence and imagination of participants. Also, by definition, from a systems perspective none encourages all participants to play an active role or encourages the inclusion of representatives from all stakeholder groups.

None of these techniques is sophisticated enough to include a mechanism for defining the network or "mess" of which the problem addressed is a part. The ask why five times technique could conceivably do so but is too loosely structured to guarantee that happening.

In the word game subcategory, a strength of lateral thinking is that it allows unlimited shifts in direction. The participant simply has to pick another random "object, animal, or color" and start again. In the attribute manipulation subcategory, more structure exists. Due to the fact, however, that the attribute lists used can always be expanded, flexibility is open-ended.

Checklist techniques in the elaboration subcategory also combine structure with an ultimately limited but large degree of flexibility. The expert consultant technique allows the user to fire and hire at will. The problems-within-problems technique obviously has limits, as does its partner, seek-the-outer-limits, which moves "outward" instead of "inward." These limits, however, will probably never be reached in most cases. In the analogy making subcategory, the only limits are those of imagination.

An obvious major weakness of all individual techniques is that they do not include an apparatus for encouraging feedback to others who might be affected by the results. When such feedback does occur, it generally concerns only one small element of the problem network. It also usually occurs in a random way, which does not ensure that all stakeholders are reached.

Further strengths include the fact that all of the techniques discussed are designed to maintain interest. Also, they all allow and encourage timely solutions. Because they are "one-shot" exercises that focus on a specific problem network piece, however, they do not encourage continuity of effort. Finally, they have no effect on implementation, unless the problem addressed is itself one of implementation.

In summary then, the general strengths of the individual-oriented problem-solving techniques are that they:

1. Encourage boldness and originality

2. Encourage flexibility and allow shifts in the direction of thought concerning the specific problem being addressed, while at the same time providing the necessary structure

3. Maintain interest over the course of the exercise

4. Allow timely solutions

The major weaknesses of these same techniques are that they:

1. Do not fully utilize the intelligence and imagination of the individuals involved

2. Do not take into account group dynamics of the stakeholder group involved

3. Focus on too small a segment of the problem network of "mess" and, therefore, do not encourage continuity

4. Do not encourage the development of an appropriate vehicle for implementation of solutions achieved

GENERAL GROUP TECHNIQUES

In the modern world of work, the individual is rarely equipped or qualified to solve problems in the most effective manner, although some executives who hang onto the "boss" mentality would strongly disagree. At the same time, the pressures experienced by a group, both internally and from external sources, are more numerous than those experienced by an individual.

The dynamics between group members themselves often creates a degree of pressure. When a group effort is undertaken, outsiders who will be affected by outcomes might also feel threatened. As a result, these outsiders might try to influence or even thwart the activities of those directly involved.

Group problem-solving techniques, therefore, must generally be more sophisticated in order to deal with these additional pressures and challenges and to encourage maximum quality input. At the same time, they must ensure that "the whole is more than the sum of its parts," i.e., that the solutions generated are more than an aggregate of individual contributions. In essence, they must be designed to generate a focused, participative, well-integrated effort.

The general group techniques have been divided into three subcategories: techniques designed specifically to generate ideas, techniques that group and/or rank ideas as well, and, finally, techniques that use competition to define the relative value of the ideas generated.

General Group Techniques that Focus on the Generation of Ideas

The purpose of these techniques is to create a cooperative atmosphere where participants involved in a group process support and feed freely off each other's attempts to generate useful ideas. The efforts of each group member help the others achieve their desired objectives.

Brainstorming

Brainstorming, developed by Alex Osborne, is probably the simplest and best-known group technique. It was designed to generate as many ideas as possible related to the problem addressed. The belief behind this technique is that the greater the number of associations produced, the less stereotypical and more creative they will be (see Figure 3.1).

Four rules are presented to the participants of a brainstorming exercise in order to create the desired cooperative atmosphere:

1. They must suspend judgment on all input, no matter what is suggested. Judgmental comments, especially criticism, must be withheld.

---

1. Present brainstorming rules to participants.

2. Write initial statement of the problem addressed on a flipchart or blackboard.

3. Solicit different versions of this problem statement from participants and write them down.

4. Have participants select the most appropriate version through discussion and vote if necessary.

5. Solicit solution-related ideas from participants, adhering to the rules, and write them down.

FIGURE 3.1   Steps in a Brainstorming Exercise

2. They must generate as many suggestions as possible without worrying about the quality of the suggestions. This will help stimulate originality.

3. Once the process has started, they must keep up the momentum by offering anything that comes into their heads.

4. They must build on ideas already produced by themselves and others, twisting them and turning them around in order to use them in any way possible.

After providing several warm-up problems to allow participants to develop a "feel" for the process and the group, the facilitator presents an integral statement of the problem at hand. Different versions of this statement are solicited and written on a blackboard or flipchart to encourage as great a variety of perspectives as possible. When no more suggested versions are forthcoming, participants choose that which is most appropriate in terms of both identifying the problem and inspiring solutions.

The next step is the generation of solution-related ideas by group members. The facilitator lists these ideas and encourages adherence to the four previously defined process rules. The facilitator is the only one allowed to question contributions and does so solely as a means of clarification.

To help generate a wider variety of ideas, participants can incorporate techniques for individuals (see previous section) into the process at different process stages. During the stage when the most appropriate problem statement is being formulated, they can use techniques that rearrange ideas or substitute similar or more specific words. During the stage in which the spectrum of ideas generated is expanded, they can use lateral thinking, forced connections, morphological analysis, or the expert consultant technique.

Operational Creativity

An alternative to brainstorming is William Gordon's operational creativity (Figure 3.2). Gordon developed this technique to deal with what he considered to be the weakness of brainstorming. Participants in a brainstorming session begin defining solutions and solution characteristics immediately. Gordon believed that this approach was too direct in that it does not encourage an adequate effort on the part of group members to explore all possible alternatives. Gordon thought that the results of such an effort would be relatively superficial.

An operational creativity session begins with only the group facilitator knowing the exact nature of the problem to be addressed. Instead of stating it, however, the facilitator asks and then writes on a board or flipchart the most general question he or she can think of that retains the essence of the problem. For example, if the problem is a faulty interdepartmental communication system, the question might be: "What are the different ways of passing information found in both the natural and mechanical worlds?"

The four rules of brainstorming are then explained. During the following idea-generating session, responses are listed on a flipchart. When

---

1. Present the same rules used in brainstorming to participants.

2. The facilitator asks the most general question possible that retains the essence of the problem addressed.

3. Brainstorming responses are listed until no more are forthcoming.

4. The facilitator then asks a more specific question which comes closer to the essence of the problem addressed, and participants respond.

5. The facilitator continues to ask increasingly specific questions, listing responses, until the actual problem at hand is addressed.

FIGURE 3.2   Steps in an Operational Creativity Exercise

no more are forthcoming, the facilitator tears the sheet of paper off the flipchart, tapes it to a wall, and begins again with a more specific question. The facilitator might ask: "How have and can these ways of communicating be fit to human social systems?"

Later questions grow increasingly specific until eventually the problem at hand is addressed. Gordon finds this roundabout approach more interesting and stimulating and believes the output generated by participants to be much richer.

Storyboard

The storyboard technique, developed by Mike Vance, combines brainstorming with a studio system for developing film plots (see Figure 3.3). The facilitator brings along a flipchart, a corkboard, thumbtacks, and a supply of five-by-eight-inch cards. The corkboard is hung in view of all participants. (Refer to the case study presented in Chapter 6 for an example of the use of the storyboard.)

The facilitator begins by describing the problem to be addressed. Participants then name potential solution categories. For example, sup-

---

1. The facilitator offers an initial version of the problem to be addressed.

2. Participants name potential solution categories which are printed on five-by-eight-inch cards and are pinned up across the top of a corkboard.

3. The facilitator asks idea-generating questions concerning each category.

4. Participants write individual answers on five-by-eight-inch cards and turn them in.

5. Answers are grouped according to common themes and pinned up under the most appropriate category card.

6. The facilitator asks further idea-generating questions based on these initial answers.

7. The idea groupings in each category are ordered by group consensus vote.

8. The three most popular ideas in each category are then expanded upon by the group leader asking further idea-generating questions.

FIGURE 3.3   Steps in a Storyboard Exercise

pose the problem is: "What should we do with the personnel who are part of an operation being shut down?" The categories might include reorientation, relocation, release, retraining, and retirement. Each category is printed on a card and the cards are pinned up at the top of the corkboard.

The facilitator then asks an idea-generating question concerning each category. For the first, it might be: "How can these employees be reoriented in a way that will profit the company?" Participants write their ideas on cards, one idea per card. The cards are collected, read aloud without naming the contributor and without criticism, grouped according to common themes, and pinned on the board under the proper category card. Depending upon what he or she sees, the facilitator asks related questions to generate more ideas.

When the process has been completed for each category, the groupings are discussed and ranked by vote. At this point, several things can occur: (1) categories or groupings can be deleted if none of the ideas contained are popular enough, (2) new categories or groupings can be formed with various idea combinations, or (3) ideas can be shifted to an entirely new category or grouping. Ideas can also be pinned up under two groupings.

If the most popular idea grouping in the "reorientation" category advances the concept of "allowing those being released to attempt to develop a new, related business," the facilitator might begin the second round of questions by asking: "What kind of support should the company provide for such a project?" He or she would frame similar questions for the three most popular groupings in each category to help define their practicality. The ensuing answers in all instances would then be called out, discussed, and listed on a flipchart sheet bearing the grouping concept as a title. When completed, these sheets would be torn off the chart and taped to a wall.

Once the 3 top idea groupings in each category have been expanded upon, the 15 "finalists" in our sample case would again be ranked by vote. The storyboard technique can utilize various individual techniques during the idea-generating part of the session.

Problem Setting

The problem setting technique focuses on developing a full and accurate problem definition (Figure 3.4). It encourages group members to gener-

---

1. The facilitator writes an initial version of the problem to be addressed on a flipchart or blackboard.

2. Participants brainstorm to identify producers, which are listed to the right of the problem.

3. Participants brainstorm to identify possible consequences and/or changes that might occur if the problem is solved. These are listed to the left of the problem.

4. Possible relationships between the individual factors in the two or three lists are explored, and lines are drawn to connect them.

5. These relationships are numerically weighted, and the various weights are written on the connecting lines.

FIGURE 3.4   Steps in a Problem Setting Exercise

ate the fullest possible range of ideas concerning both problem producers and problem consequences. It helps those taking part to better understand each other's viewpoints and develop a consensus. Such elaboration and consensus, in turn, help suggest more comprehensive and universally acceptable solutions.

The group facilitator of a problem setting exercise writes an initial version of the problem in the middle of a flipchart sheet. Group members then suggest possible problem producers. These are listed to the right of the problem. Brainstorming as well as various other individual techniques can be used to define these producers.

Once the initial list is recorded, the group facilitator can expand it by asking participants to define "second-level" producers. For example, if the problem is declining productivity, an originally defined producer might be lack of worker commitment. When asked to suggest "second-level" producers responsible for this lack of worker commitment, participants might offer boring work, lack of appropriate incentives, or bad management attitude.

During the second phase of the problem setting exercise, group members are required to suggest possible problem consequences or, as an alternative, the changes they think might occur in their individual situations if the problem were solved. These suggestions are listed by the group facilitator to the left of the problem. For example, a possible consequence of declining productivity might be layoffs. One change that might occur if the problem were solved could be salary raises. A third approach would be to list both consequences and changes, allowing participants to view and compare their two possible futures.

The third phase of the problem setting exercise includes an exploration by group members of the relationships that exist between individual factors in the three lists. Lines can be drawn to connect related factors. Comparative numerical weights can be assigned to these relationships and written above the connecting lines as a means of defining the central issues. This third phase could be considered a sophisticated form of preferential listing or establishing priorities. The accompanying discussion will also help identify areas where adequate information is lacking.

Refer to the case study presented in Chapter 6 for an example of how a team employed some of these techniques to define its problem and write a problem statement.

General Group Techniques that Focus on Defining Priorities

The last two techniques discussed in the previous subcategory include grouping and/or ranking. Idea generation, however, rather than idea grouping or idea ranking was their central objective. Their strength was the raw number of ideas they could produce. In contrast, the strengths of the techniques described in this subcategory are (1) their ability to facilitate the building of a useful network of ideas concerning a specific problem and/or (2) their ability to define the group's opinion concerning the relative merit of an idea.

The purpose of the techniques described in this subcategory, therefore, is to again create a cooperative atmosphere, but this time one in which participants in a problem-solving process support and feed freely off each other's efforts so as to successfully group and order useful ideas. The efforts of each group member again help the others achieve their desired objective.

The TKJ technique (described next) is an elaboration of the individual technique that uses grouping. The nominal group technique is an elaboration of preferential listing. The cause-and-effect or fishbone diagram and modified Delphi techniques, in turn, combine the strengths of both the TKJ and nominal group techniques.

TKJ

TKJ is a technique developed by Kobayashi and Kawakita (Figure 3.5). Its purpose is to synthesize different perspectives into a definition acceptable to all process participants. It can be used in separate exercises to elaborate on the nature of a problem and to elaborate on the nature of potential solutions to this problem.

TKJ is led by a facilitator. The required props are a flipchart or blackboard and a supply of five-by-eight-inch cards. As a first step, the facilitator describes and then writes on the board or chart an initial version of the problem to be addressed. Participants then individually list

---

1. The group facilitator writes an initial version of the problem to be addressed on a flipchart or blackboard.

2. Participants list important and objectively verifiable problem- or solution-related facts on five-by-eight-inch cards.

3. The cards are collected and redistributed so that no participant receives his or her own.

4. A randomly chosen participant reads aloud a fact from one of his or her cards. The fact is recorded on the flipchart or blackboard by the group facilitator.

5. Other participants read related facts aloud from their cards. These are added to the list headed by the initial fact.

6. When one round has been completed, another is begun with the reading of another fact by another randomly chosen participant.

7. Other participants again read aloud related facts which are added to that list.

8. When all facts have been assigned to a set, participants choose a name for each set that reflects its essence and write the name on a card. If more than one alternative is generated, the choice can be made by vote.

9. Set names are then distributed and the process is repeated. Someone randomly chosen reads a set name, and others add related set names to the list. Someone else reads another set name, and so on.

10. The cycle continues until only one all-inclusive set name card remains.

FIGURE 3.5   Steps in a TKJ Exercise

problem- or solution-related facts on separate cards. These facts must be important and objectively verifiable.

For example, suppose the initial version of the problem for a computer firm is falling sales in the Philadelphia area. Relevant facts that are objectively verifiable might include: (1) salespeople are not covering all possible targets, (2) another computer firm is focusing its marketing resources on the Philadelphia area, (3) a new complex of information-based industries is growing just outside the city limits, (4) the sales force in this area has recently been cut, and (5) the marketing budget for this region is relatively low in terms of expected sales.

As a second step, the fact cards are collected and redistributed so that no participant receives his or her own. The facilitator then randomly picks a participant and asks that person to read one of his or her facts out loud. Others are encouraged to offer facts related to this initial one from their cards, thus building a set. For example, if fact 3 from our example concerning the computer firm in Philadelphia is read first, facts 1 and 4 might fit with it into one set. Then the facilitator picks another participant to read a fact out loud. Again, others with related facts on their cards add them to build a set. This process continues until all of the facts have been incorporated into one of the sets.

The next step is for participants to choose a name for each set that reflects its essence. This name is written on a new card. Set names are then distributed and the process is repeated with them. The facilitator picks a participant to read one of his or her set names. Then others add related set names to build a set name set, and so on. This type of synthetic group activity continues until one all-inclusive set name card containing one all-inclusive problem definition or solution is obtained.

Nominal Group Technique

The nominal group technique (Figure 3.6) is in many ways similar to TKJ. Its focus, however, is on establishing priorities rather than synthesizing. The technique was developed by Andrew Van De Ven and Andre Delbecq. Their purpose was to encourage the useful participation of all group members in a problem-solving situation. The nominal group technique requires that participants contribute ideas, but in a way that initially nullifies the constraints of challenge and possible domination by others. At the same time, it provides a system for critiquing and selecting

---

1. The facilitator writes an initial version of the problem to be addressed on a flipchart or blackboard.

2. Participants write their ideas concerning solutions on a piece of paper.

3. Each participant reads aloud one idea, which is written down, then a second after other group members have contributed, until all ideas are recorded on the flipchart or blackboard.

4. The ideas are briefly discussed and clarified.

5. Participants then rank the ideas and turn their results in to the facilitator.

6. Votes are recorded on the flipchart or blackboard and voting pattern inconsistencies discussed.

7. A final individual listing in terms of priorities is made by participants, turned in, and recorded on the flipchart or blackboard.

FIGURE 3.6   Steps in a Nominal Group Technique Exercise

between ideas, which again limits confrontation and encourages well-considered contributions.

The process begins with an impartial facilitator posing to the group a question that indicates the nature of the problem to be defined or solved. The question must be carefully designed. It is a good idea to pretest it. Participants are told to silently list their ideas concerning answers on a piece of paper. Each group member then reads one of his or her ideas aloud. The ideas are recorded, still without discussion, on a flipchart. When one round is completed, a second is begun, and so on, until all ideas are recorded.

Each idea is then briefly discussed and clarified if necessary. Participants can voice agreement of disagreement at this point, but drawn out debates are not allowed. The next step is for participants to silently write the ideas they think are most important or worthwhile on individual five-by-eight-inch cards. Then, participants order these cards and turn them in to the facilitator, who records the votes on the flipchart. When this tabulation is completed, the results are discussed and voting pattern inconsistencies are examined. Following the discussion, priorities are finalized by another session of writing priorities on five-by-eight-inch cards.

Cause-and-Effect or Fishbone Diagram

The fishbone diagram is one of the simplest techniques available for identifying and organizing the causes of a problem in terms of sequence or priority. It was developed by Ishikawa and is usually grouped with statistical productivity measuring techniques because it complements them so well.

The fishbone technique is based on a pictorial representation of the issue addressed. The representation is in the shape of a fish skeleton. The head of the fish is the problem or the desired improvement. The spine is the major cause of the problem or the major step necessary to accomplish the desired improvement. The bones running off the spine are contributing factors to the major producer or supporting steps to the major step. Smaller bones might also angle off the main bones to represent subfactors or substeps. Even smaller bones might angle off those, and so on.

If there is more than one major cause, it is necessary to create more than one skeleton with the same head but different spines. It is also possible that one of the bones/factors might eventually replace the spine as the major cause or step. This change could result from participants' increased understanding of the situation.

The fishbone diagram can be used to show sequence. The bone closest to the head represents the first factor. It can also be used to show priority. The closer to the head a bone lies, the higher its priority as a cause.

Suppose the problem is low productivity. The spine of the fishbone diagram might initially be inappropriate use of technology. The bones that extend from the spine could include lack of maintenance on existing equipment, lack of corporate reinvestment in technology, lack of research into technological improvements and new technologies, lack of appropriate long-range technological planning, and lack of a vehicle that allows employees to suggest ways to improve current technology.

Angle bones off the bone representing lack of research might include lack of facilities for research, lack of funds for research, and lack of staff for research.

Participants might also decide that the spine for the problem of low productivity should actually be "lack of appropriate long-range planning" and that a bone angling off this spine should be labeled "inappropriate use of technology." Thus, a new fishbone diagram would evolve, using many of the same causes but arranging them differently.

Refer to the case study presented in Chapter 6 for an example of how a team utilized a fishbone diagram to determine the root cause of its problem in Step 6 of its Quality Journey.

Modified Delphi

The modified Delphi technique for smaller groups is another means of gathering related information to clarify the nature of a problem and to suggest comprehensive solutions (Figure 3.7). It can be considered a synthesis of the TKJ and nominal group techniques in that it both groups characteristics and ranks groupings. Its uniqueness is that participants do not meet each other until the mid-point of the process, if at all.

Again the exercise begins with a facilitator presenting the problem to be addressed in the form of a question. Participants privately list problem-related factors they consider relevant to or part of the solution on a sheet of paper. The facilitator collects and synthesizes these individual lists, culling out or combining repetitious items.

The resulting master list is then presented to group members, who privately divide the factors into classifications on a second sheet of paper. The results are again collected, organized, and redistributed so that participants can decide either privately or through discussion which cat-

---

1. A facilitator presents the problem to be addressed to participants.

2. Participants privately list problem-related factor or answers.

3. The lists are collected by the facilitator and combined into one nonrepetitive list which is distributed to the participants.

4. Participants privately divide the items in this "master" list into categories.

5. The results are collected, combined, and redistributed. The combining in this case can be done either by the group leader or by participants in the group.

6. Participants privately rank the categories decided upon.

7. The results are recorded and discussed in a group session.

FIGURE 3.7   Steps in a Modified Delphi Exercise

egories are repetitious and which are the most relevant. It is preferable that decisions to be reached through consensus; if this is not possible, the majority rules.

The final step is for group members to privately order the categories according to their own feelings on a third sheet of paper. These lists of priorities are collected by the leader and totaled. The results can then be written on a flipchart and discussed. If, during this phase, the facilitator feels that opinion is shifting significantly, he or she can repeat the part of the exercise in which priorities are established.

General Group Techniques that Introduce Competition

All of the group techniques discussed thus far are designed to encourage cooperation. Some establish rules that outlaw competition or conflict. Others simply do not allow any judgmental interaction to occur. Groups that use these techniques might eventually rank ideas, but in a nonaggressive manner.

In this subcategory, however, two radically different techniques are introduced. They actually incorporate competition as a means of (1) encouraging greater effort by process participants and (2) defining more accurately the relative strengths of the alternative solutions generated.

The theory behind this approach is that a competitive atmosphere makes participants try harder. It stimulates more originality and a greater degree of discernment in problem-solving efforts than does cooperation. The question of whether or not such a theory is, in fact, supported by experimental evidence remains unanswered. Some experiments show that it does, while others indicate that cooperation is the best alternative. It is likely that the personality types of the participants play a major role in the outcome.

Dialectic

The first technique that incorporates competition is the dialectic (Figure 3.8). Developed by West Churchman, it is used mainly to identify the assumptions on which the most holistic, effective solution can be based in a group problem-solving situation. The key participant is a "decision maker" who must be acceptable to everyone else involved.

1. A "decision maker" forms two or more teams from exercise participants and provides each with a problem statement and relevant information.

2. The teams are assigned conflicting sides of an issue, generate answers representing these sides, and present them to the group as a whole.

3. The decision maker, or a third team, creates a synthesis and defends it before the teams representing conflicting sides, with the decision maker acting as referee.

FIGURE 3.8   Steps in a Dialectic Exercise

The first step in the process is for the decision maker to form two or more teams from the group participants. The decision maker supplies the teams with the same problem statement and, when possible, with relevant information. The teams then formulate individual solutions. The decision maker can also predefine the objectives and/or approaches of the different teams. For example, if the problem is to decide whether or not an oil company should buy a shipping line, one team would be instructed to support the purchase and the other to oppose it.

In this example, the two teams would probably generate most of their own information. Also, the decision maker would probably be a collection of top-level executives, or a board of directors, rather than a single individual.

The dialectic can also be used as a follow-up to other group techniques. A problem-solving exercise could begin with brainstorming, storyboard, TKJ, or modified Delphi. In cases where more than one attractive alternative materializes, the dialectic would be introduced to define the most appropriate choice. Obviously, the various alternatives would have supporters who would be assigned to the appropriate teams.

After all arguments have been heard, the decision maker in a dialectic exercise traditionally creates a synthesis, developing his or her own set of assumptions from which an effective solution can be generated.

A modification to the process would be for a third or fourth team to act as the synthesizer. Once this additional team has defined its assumptions, it would be asked to defend them before the two or three original teams. The decision maker would referee this final exchange and settle any disagreements that threatened ultimate consensus.

Swapping

The second technique in this category, a modification of the dialectic developed by Roth, is called swapping (Figure 3.9). It is most valuable in situations where participants in a problem-solving exercise have generated two extremely different and/or irreconcilable solutions or sets of assumptions upon which a solution is to be based.

The breakdown of conflicting opinions is usually according to frame of reference. For example, the problem facing a beer manufacturer and distributor might be how best to dispel a nasty rumor about product ingredients started by a rival company. Representatives from the finance department, with cost foremost in their minds, might believe that the best and cheapest solution is personal contact (e.g., salespeople should take the time necessary to personally deny the rumor and calm any fears key clients might have). Representatives from the sales department, on the other hand, concerned about the added workload and the uncertainty of such an approach, might strongly support a more expensive advertising campaign.

Once the arguments have been fully developed and a state of impasse reached, the swapping technique is brought into play. A referee is assigned, and the swap is made. The two sets of combatants are instructed to develop a 30-minute or longer presentation of the opposition's argument, adding at least two new supportive points or solution ideas.

---

1. Participants are divided into teams based upon their opposing solutions to the problem to be addressed.

2. A referee is assigned.

3. The teams are instructed to develop a 30-minute or longer presentation of the opposition's argument, adding at least two new points or solution ideas.

4. The referee decides whether or not the presentations are adequate.

5. If they are not, the referee can force the teams to reorganize and re-present as many times as he or she thinks necessary.

6. Each presentation acceptable to the referee is critiqued by the other teams.

7. Once all teams have made acceptable presentations, another attempt is made to achieve a solution that is acceptable to all sides.

FIGURE 3.9   Steps in a Swapping Exercise

They must put themselves in the shoes of their opponents. In order to facilitate development of the necessary mindset, they are given access to any information requested, unless the referee deems it irrelevant.

If the referee decides that a presentation is insincere or does not adequately address the proposed solution, he or she can force the team to reorganize and re-present as many times as necessary. When the referee finally approves the team offerings, each presentation is critiqued by the other teams. Finally, another attempt is made to achieve synthesis.

This approach has the following strengths: (1) it is educational and broadens the perspective of participants in problem-solving exercises; (2) because of the different frames of reference introduced, the opposition's solution might be strengthened; and (3) because of the broadened perspectives of all participants, an acceptable synthesis might now be possible, whereas before it was not.

A possible weakness of the approach is that participants might not take it seriously. In such cases, whether or not top-level management supports the referee in his or her decisions may be the determining factor.

Evaluation of General Group Techniques

The general group techniques defined here begin with the least sophisticated and progress to the most sophisticated. We began with those designed simply to generate the greatest number of ideas concerning a problem or desired improvement and proceeded to techniques which generate ideas and identify common themes that run through them. The third level included techniques which generate ideas, identify themes, and then define the relative value of those themes through ranking. The fourth set introduced the element of competition in order to excite efforts and, in swapping, to help clarify the opposition's viewpoint.

All of the general group techniques encourage boldness and originality. They go much further toward utilizing the intelligence and imagination of participants than do the individual techniques discussed earlier. They encourage all participants to play an active role in the problem-solving process and allow the inclusion of representatives from all stakeholder groups, although, with the possible exception of the modified Delphi technique, they do not generally require it.

Again, most of these techniques are problem specific and do not force participants to pay attention to the problem network or "mess" of which the problem addressed is a part. One exception might be the fishbone diagram, which allows and can encourage the necessary exploration. Due to this same focus on an individual problem, very few of the general group techniques can be considered truly flexible. All provide continuous feedback and, with the possible exception of the modified Delphi, all provide timely decisions.

Because these techniques are problem specific and are used in "one-shot" exercises, they do not encourage continuity of effort. Neither do they provide a vehicle for implementation of results.

In summary, the strengths of the general group techniques are that they:

1. Encourage boldness and originality

2. Utilize the intelligence and imagination of participants

3. Encourage participants to play an active role

4. Take group dynamics into account

5. Encourage flexibility in terms of the problem addressed

6. Maintain interest over the course of the exercise

7. Allow timely solutions

Their weaknesses are that they:

1. Do not force the participation of representatives from all stake-holder groups

2. Focus on a small segment of the problem network and, therefore, do not encourage flexibility or continuity in terms of the network as a whole

3. Do not encourage development of an appropriate vehicle for the implementation of solutions

SYSTEMS-ORIENTED GROUP TOOLS AND TECHNIQUES

The tools and techniques described in this section are used mainly in situations where problems are known to exist but have been defined only in the most general terms. They are also used in situations where organizations are trying to identify/address a suspected network of problems rather than focus initially on one or several problems. Their similarity is that they all adopt a holistic perspective in terms of the system addressed. Instead of simply being compatible with, they are capable of and quite frequently absorb the previously defined individual and group techniques.

Two basic types of systemic tools and techniques are presented. The first type includes the flowchart tool and the two words and breaking the ice techniques, which are used solely to help identify the problems in a network. The second type defines the force field analysis, idealized design, and modified idealized design techniques. Its main purpose is to discover solutions to problem networks. Only the last technique discussed, the search conference, addresses both tasks.

Flowchart

This first systemic tool is used to generate a frame of reference within which a network of organization-, unit-, or system-wide problems can be more easily identified. A flowchart can be a diagram, especially when a manufacturing process is being charted. More commonly, however, it is a straightforward, comprehensive list of steps involved in a process. The trick is not to leave anything out. Once the list is complete, participants look for problem areas within the defined process steps and within the gaps between these steps. They then develop clear definitions of the problems involved and use other techniques to deal with them.

Refer to the case study presented in Chapter 6 for an example of how a team constructed a flowchart in Step 4 of its Quality Journey to document the existing process in its designated problem area. After introducing and verifying the effectiveness of its solution, the team revised the flowchart as part of standardizing the new work process in Step 10. The flowchart was useful in understanding the process as well as identifying areas for measurement.

The example provided in Figure 3.10 is a flowchart developed by the work services unit affiliated with a rehabilitation center. The unit tries to employ handicapped people, frequently those who have spent time in the rehabilitation center, to complete relatively simple tasks which they are capable of completing, such as packing pieces into boxes or changing labels on equipment. The unit accepts a wide variety of jobs from a constantly shifting range of companies. Obviously, it needs to remain extremely flexible while at the same time maintaining control.

1. Review nature of work requested by potential client
   A. Do we have necessary expertise?
   B. What are the customers' requirements?
      - Quality
      - Turnaround time
      - Date customer could make components available

2. Time study and methodology study for job
   A. Determination of need for "fixtures"

3. Discussion of project with production department
   A. Establishment of tentative schedule
   B. Consideration of labor hours available
   C. Consideration of need to hire additional personnel

4. Development of bid price; presentation of written bid and terms to customer

5. Notification of acceptance of bid by customer

6. Confirmation of production schedule and required turnaround time

7. Recruitment of additional manpower when necessary

8. Construction of fixtures, if necessary

9. Make arrangements for incoming materials

10. Receive incoming materials (shipping department)
    A. Verify counts
    B. Log inventory into process control system

11. If discrepancies noted, notify customer to resolve

12. Compare incoming materials to samples

13. Make sure enough pieces are available to complete actual order

14. Using actual materials, verify time study, review price and methodology

15. Issue production order; issue purchase order for any necessary equipment

16. Write step-by-step procedures

17. Assign and enter job step codes into process control system

18. Enter production order and any purchase orders involved into process control system

19. Give production department copies of all written information (receiving information, step codes, purchase orders, time studies, etc.)

FIGURE 3.10   Flowchart for Procurement Process

The flowchart was developed jointly by the functional managers and the work services director. The group opted to start with the procurement process and to chart the entire operation through to shipping. Only that segment of the flowchart exercise dealing with procurement is presented in Figure 3.10.

Two Words

The two words technique was used at Paul Revere Insurance Group and is described by Pat Townsend in his book *Commit to Quality*. The process begins with the unit involved as a whole describing what it does in just two words, one verb and one noun. Offerings are written on a flipchart and then discussed and debated until a consensus is reached.

The unit is then broken down by function. Representatives from each function write on three-by-five-inch cards all the things they do in just two words, one verb and one noun. Once this part of the exercise is completed, the cards for each function are laid out on a large table or on the floor and are linked to see what the relationships are, whether or not the tasks complement each other, and where they might overlap.

If any of the cards do not fit into the chains formed, the participants ask: "Why not?" The possibility that they might actually belong in another function is explored, as well as the possibility that they are not necessary.

Breaking the Ice

This technique was developed and is used extensively by Roth. It borrows heavily from Fred Emery's search conference, which is discussed at the end of this chapter. Breaking the ice is used with groups or teams that represent one function. It cannot be used with cross-functional teams for reasons that will become apparent.

Breaking the ice begins with a facilitator asking participants to identify trends in the general community which affect their ability to do their jobs the way they want to do them. This technique allows the participants to get to know each other by talking about something that is in no way threatening. It gives them a chance to warm up to the situation rather than staring suspiciously at the facilitator. All contributions are listed on flipchart sheets, which are taped up in order on a wall.

After these contributions have been discussed and the participants are a little more comfortable with both the process and the facilitator, the next challenge thrown out is: "Now let's identify trends in our organization which affect your ability to do your job the way you want to do it."

An obvious modern-day example of such a trend would be downsizing. Another would be the willingness or unwillingness of managers to communicate with each other and with employees. There are two parts to this question—organization-wide trends and trends within a function/department. The facilitator starts with organization-wide trends, but the team usually moves without prompting into function/departmental trends.

After these trends are listed and discussed, the facilitator asks participants to list their job responsibilities, not necessarily in order. This phase could be viewed as a disorganized but much quicker form of the flowchart exercise.

Once this list is complete, the team is asked to brainstorm and to begin suggesting ways they think any system on any level of the organization can be improved. For example, many teams talk about the need to improve the message system in their office, while others present the current organization-wide shift system as a possible project.

Teams are encouraged to define issues relating to products, production processes, management systems, and the work environment. Nothing is sacred. The facilitator's main responsibilities during this phase are to ask clarifying questions, not let participants get immediately involved in solving the individual problems identified, and to make sure that the definition of each problem as listed is clear.

Once no more issues are forthcoming, the facilitator goes back to the list of trends in the community which affect the employees' ability to do their jobs the way they want to do them and to the list of employee responsibilities. The facilitator leads team members slowly through these lists to make sure nothing has been missed.

Once the list of potential improvements is completed, at least for the moment, the facilitator asks the participants to divide the usually 30 or 40 items into 3 categories:

1. In-house issues which can be addressed without involving anyone outside the function—This might include bad lighting or improving the filing system.

2. Border issues on which participants must work in conjunction with another function—A common one is bad parts or information coming down the line.

Environmental Trends that Affect My Ability to Do My Job the Way I Want to Do It
1. Loss of jobs due to old companies moving out
2. Crime on the rise
3. Influx of unskilled labor
4. Loss of pride in city
5. Deteriorating neighborhoods
6. Increase in drug-related activity
7. Rising taxes
8. New industries require new skills but training unavailable
9. City lacks plan/direction
10. Homes being turned into apartments
11. ****

Organizational Trends that Affect My Ability to Do My Job the Way I Want to Do It
1. Policies change without my knowing or being asked for input
2. Threat of layoffs
3. Unwillingness to invest in needed technology
4. Managers frequently do not communicate well
5. Often hard to get needed information
6. Frequently get calls that have nothing to do with our department
7. Lack of necessary training or cross-training
8. Departments do not know what other departments do
9. Do not know where files are when someone is using them
10. Phone directory often confusing
11. ****

FIGURE 3.11   Breaking the Ice Technique Used in Secretarial Function (** indicates list is abbreviated)

3. Organization-wide issues that affect policy or involve expenditure of a large amount of money and, therefore, must involve upper-level management—This could include the need for a new process control system or more staff.

Once the issues are properly categorized, the facilitator encourages but does not force participants to pick the easiest in-house issues to work on first, in order to produce quick results. This allows the team to experience success early in the process, so that team members can prove to

Function Job Responsibilities
1. Help integrate activities of department
2. Word processing
3. Filing
4. Answering queries
5. Coordinating with other departments
6. Keeping master schedules
7. Photocopying
8. ****

Projects to Improve Operation (Categorized as Level 1, 2, 3)
1. Develop system for users to write names on a tab when removing files from cabinet (1)
2. Improve intercom system (3)
3. Central library for records (3)
4. Link all computers (2)
5. Cross-train within office (1)
6. Make copiers more accessible (2)
7. Bring someone in from information systems function to answer questions (2)
8. Set up employee education program so we can learn what other departments do (3)
9. Rearrange offices to make work flow easier (1)
10. Revise in-house phone directory (2)
11. ****

themselves that they are capable of creating change and so that teams can prove to upper-level managers who are watching that they can move rapidly and effectively.

This technique was used as part of an effort to improve the operations of a middle-sized city government. The lists presented in Figure 3.11 were generated by the secretarial team.

Force Field Analysis

Force field analysis, developed by Kurt Lewin, begins by identifying two diametrically opposed sets of social forces which exert pressure on any

Current situation:	Work force morale deteriorating
Ideal situation:	All employees 100 percent committed to doing their best
Worst possible situation:	Employees strike

Restraining Forces	Driving Forces
Recent downsizing	Stable work force
Added responsibilities	Cross-training
Managers who don't listen	New quality process
Lack of opportunity for employee advancement	Management's promise of no more layoffs
Poor downward communication	New computerized technology
Recent pay increases for highest levels	Beginnings of team approach to production

FIGURE 3.12   Listing Example of Force Field Analysis Restraining and Driving Forces

sociotechnical system. Lewin contends that "restraining forces" are those forces that continually are pushing the current situation toward the worst possible outcome. "Driving forces" are those forces that are continually pushing it toward the best possible outcome. The objective of a force field analysis exercise is to identify the members of both sets in a specific situation and their relationships (Figure 3.12). Once this is done, participants must find ways to reduce the number and power of the relevant restraining forces while at the same time increasing the number and power of the relevant driving forces.

Refer to the case study presented in Chapter 6 for an example of how a team employed force field analysis to plan for potential difficulties in Step 9 of its Quality Journey.

In order to complete this exercise, the following six questions must be addressed:

1. What is the current situation, what would the ideal situation be, and what could the worst possible situation be?

2. What are the restraining forces which are pushing the current situation toward the worst possible alternative?

3. What are the driving forces which are pushing the current situation toward the ideal state?

4. What relationship exists between these two sets of forces?

5. Over which restraining and driving forces do we believe we have influence, and which of these are important now?

6. For each of the restraining and driving forces subject to our influence, what are specific action steps the group can take to eliminate or strengthen them?

In generating the answers to Questions 2 and 3, the following previously defined techniques might be used: expert consultant applied by the group as a whole, brainstorming, storyboard, nominal group technique, and modified Delphi. In generating answers to the three parts of Question 1, TKJ can be added to this list. Definition of the ideal situation can also be achieved through the use of the idealized design and the what/why/ how techniques described next. Inclusion of these latter two techniques, however, in a force field analysis exercise would cause it to be extremely time consuming.

Once identified, the forces should be listed on a flipchart, with arrows indicating whether they are restraining of driving forces. Question 5 is addressed by circling those forces which can be influenced. Participants might also rank the forces, prioritizing them in terms of the relative ease with which they can be influenced beneficially.

Finally, as a means of identifying the "specific action steps" cited in Question 6, Lewin introduces a checklist of further questions to be addressed:

1. Who will do what?

2. What exactly will be done?

3. Where will it be carried out?

4. When will it be done?

5. How will it be augmented?

This is the old "newspaper reporter" checklist adapted to the workplace. In terms of workplace problem solving, however, the "what" question should probably be addressed first. This change will allow the participants to address the other questions in a more effective manner.

Idealized Design

Idealized design was developed by Russell Ackoff as part of the interactive planning paradigm. It is used primarily in comprehensive efforts to plan the future of entire organizations. It can, however, also be used in simpler problem-solving exercises, as it was in the Bell Labs project where Ackoff first encountered it. Idealized design twists conventional logic around. Traditionally, when faced with a problem, we carefully define where we are, or what the weaknesses of our current approach or system are. We then prioritize these weaknesses and work on improving them individually. (Refer to the case study presented in Chapter 6 for an example of how a team employed this concept to develop additional solutions during Step 9 of its Quality Journey.)

Idealized design, instead of starting where we are and trying to move forward in an often piecemeal fashion, begins by addressing the question of where we would *like to be* ideally, where we should be, and works backward from that point. In other words, instead of defining existing constraints to change and striving to identify the best way to manipulate or overcome these constraints in terms of current conditions and environmental trends, groups utilizing idealization begin by defining what they would consider to be the ideal state. Once consensus is reached on this ideal state, the groups develop plans for bridging the gaps between their current reality and the ideal state, prioritize the involved activities, and then generate action plans.

The major strength of the idealized design technique is its systemic nature. It starts by identifying a comprehensive whole which is desired and then molds the pieces of the system in terms of that whole, rather than shaping individual pieces and then trying to fit them together in a way that builds a meaningful whole.

Idealized design, as noted, is most frequently used when addressing larger, more systemic problems. Moving a filing cabinet would hardly necessitate this technique, unless process participants begin to suspect that the misplaced filing cabinet is part of a larger, office design issue.

Problem-solving exercises begin with the total destruction of the system addressed. Once it is destroyed, participants are told to redesign the system in any way they wish.

The first step in this process is to decide what the system ought to produce or do ideally, ignoring factors, such as corporate policy, which might inhibit change. Next, participants identify characteristics that would be necessary to the system if it were to achieve the ideal state. The third step is to actually design the new system, getting down to shaping the nuts and bolts which would allow the desired characteristics to materialize. Next, participants define action steps necessary for implementation of the design elements. Finally, participants decide which of the action steps are possible in terms of their current reality and, then, which steps should be priorities.

The key to the success of this approach is for those involved to develop a clear target to aim for and one to which everyone agrees. Once the target is spelled out in terms of characteristics and design elements, efforts are planned that will move the group, sometimes slowly, toward the target. Another strength of the approach is that once the current reality has been adequately "destroyed," imaginative thinking is encouraged. The technique can be presented as a cooperative group game or a fantasy exercise, the results of which threaten no one. Usually, participants begin to understand the full value and power of the technique only when they start working on the actual system design elements and realize that the gap between their reality and the ideal is not as wide as first imagined.

Results of an idealized design exercise must meet the following criteria:

1. They must be technologically feasible. The design cannot incorporate nonexistent technology or technology that is not cost effective. For example, a steel-producing facility powered entirely by solar energy is not technologically feasible at this time.

2. The system designed must be capable of surviving in the current internal/external economy.

3. The system designed must include or be linked to an apparatus that allows constant revision based on the continual learning of employees.

As an example of a successful idealized design exercise, consider the following scenario of a luxury resort situated on the west coast of Mexico. The surrounding region was extremely poor. Two problems were presented: (1) the company wanted to attract foreign vacationers, especially from the United States, and (2) the company wanted to control the local population. Natives were mugging tourists and destroying resort property. Townspeople who had been given jobs by the company were not delivering services with the appropriate attitude. They were often sullen and uncontrollable, even when threatened with dismissal.

The company had reacted to this hostile environment by donating a new jail as well as funds to increase the local police force. It had built a wall around the resort compound. Caddies on the golf course had been trained to double as bodyguards.

The first step taken by the consultants hired by the company was to survey people from the United States who had previously vacationed abroad. They were asked to describe the atmosphere they sought. The number one priority they defined was to have contact with the local culture. The number two priority was a safe environment.

With these two requirements in mind, the consultants then spent time at the resort. What they found was a closed environment—guests ate at the resort, used the private beach, and were entertained by the staff. The town adjacent to the resort was relatively uninteresting. The few small restaurants in the town catered to local residents, and there was little for tourists to buy in the way of crafts, indigenous clothing, or other goods. Streets were dirty, and buildings were run down and unattractive. The landscape was mainly dry brush with a few trees. The two major sources of income were subsistence farming and fishing. The resort bought none of its food locally.

The townspeople interviewed by the consultants resented the resort and its constant display of wealth. It rapidly became obvious that if the resort owners wanted to improve the attitude of local inhabitants and at the same time encourage customer contact with the local culture, they needed to change their approach.

The next step was to redefine the problem(s). A team was formed, made up of the people involved. They framed their ideal state as a question: "How could the company develop a resort operation that would attract U.S. tourists and prove profitable not only to the company, but also to the local community and to the region as a whole?"

Design characteristics needed to achieve this ideal state included:

1. Clean up the town and make it more attractive.

2. Develop a marketplace in the town that would cater to tourists.

3. Develop a crafts manufacturing complex that would take advantage of the region's reputation for wood carving, pottery, and

weaving. Invite tourists into the complex to watch the craftspeople at work and perhaps to take lessons.

4. Encourage local farmers to raise materials used by the craftspeople, such as gourds, reeds/grasses, wood, and leather. Support and coordinate their efforts.

5. Mount or support a government project to reforest the surrounding hills with hybrid trees that could survive in the local climate.

6. Mount or support an effort to plant shrubbery and grasses for livestock to feed on and to prevent erosion.

7. Use the skills of local fishermen to help make game fishing a major attraction for resort guests.

Design elements defined as necessary to turn the desired design characteristics into reality included:

1. The company should establish a department for regional development. Its purpose would be to provide an interface between company operations and regional inhabitants. It would:

   ■ Conduct necessary surveys and research

   ■ Define what the region might be capable of supplying

   ■ Match the cost of developing these capabilities against long-term benefits

   ■ Seek government and private funding for projects that seem cost effective

2. A series of town meetings should be held, where ideas generated by the idealization team would be presented and input would be sought from local residents.

3. A joint committee of town leaders and resort managers should be formed to oversee the activities of the department for regional development.

Modified Idealized Design

The concept of idealized design can also be used in smaller projects. As mentioned, the only requirement is that the project deal with a system. For example, suppose members of a factory maintenance department are having trouble hanging onto their tools. The smaller ones tend to disappear and the bigger ones cannot be found when needed. Tools are left lying all over the plant. The company buys and supplies tools to maintenance workers but is unhappy about the expense involved.

The workers expressed the problem as follows: "We don't want to have to spend half the day running around looking for tools or standing in line at the supply cage to get new ones." When asked to define the ideal arrangement, they eventually came up with: "Tools available immediately when we need them." When asked what characteristics such a system would have, they identified the following:

1. The company should issue each worker one set of small tools that could be carried on a belt or in a toolbox.

2. The company should provide a safe place for employees to leave tools when not using them.

3. The large tools should be kept together in one place when not being used and should be returned to that place after use.

Design elements eventually included the following:

1. Maintenance men should buy the small tools themselves. The company should pay for the first set. The company should replace them only if broken. Otherwise, the employees should replace them.

2. The company should provide each worker with a locker in which to store tools.

3. The company should fence the locker area in and lock it up at night to prevent theft.

4. The large tools should be kept in a large chest that can be moved to big jobs. Workers who take tools from the chest are responsible for replacing them.

5. If a large tool is missing, work orders should be checked to determine who used the tool last.

6. The chest should be left in the fenced in area at night and should also be locked.

Search Conference

The search conference technique, developed by Fred Emery, is the most global. Rather than addressing the problematic system directly, it starts by exploring the containing environment of the system, thus encouraging a broader perspective. The objective of the technique is to help participants (1) develop a shared perception, (2) define a mutually desired future, and (3) identify ways of achieving that future.

The process can be shaped in several different ways, largely depending upon the nature and size of the organization and group involved. A stock set of stages exists, and stages can be chosen based on the situation. The stages can also be modified.

As an example, a search conference was conducted for a coin-operated equipment service company attempting to reorganize and improve the effectiveness and profitability of its operation. Representatives from all major functions and all different levels were included.

The process began with participants identifying general trends in the United States that they considered important. Next, they identified trends in the United States that they considered to be important to their specific industry. The third stage included an oral history of the coin-operated service industry. The fourth stage included a history of the company outlined by the president. The fifth stage was a reference scenario in which participants described a probable future for the organization in both financial and nonfinancial terms if current trends did not change.

The sixth stage focused on the generation of a "desirable future." Here participants defined and listed the ideal characteristics they would like to see their organization develop. These characteristics were then grouped according to three common themes: growth, customer relations, and organization design.

Finally, in the seventh stage, design elements which gave the organization the desired characteristics were generated for each theme sector. The sixth and seventh stages obviously incorporated aspects of idealization. The next step was for participants to begin planning implementation of the design elements.

Evaluation of Systems-Oriented Group Tools and Techniques

These tools and techniques are not designed for use in individual problem-solving efforts or focused group problem-solving efforts. They are based on the belief that no problem stands alone, that each belongs to a network or "mess," and that because of this, no matter how effectively the original problem is addressed, the desired results will probably not be realized due to constraints that exist elsewhere in the network.

The systems-oriented tools and techniques are broken down into two classifications. The first includes the flowchart and two words and breaking the ice techniques, which are used to help identify the problems in the network as well as their interdependencies. The second classification includes force field analysis, idealized design, modified idealized design, and the search conference, which are used mainly to dissolve problem networks.

With the possible exception of the flowchart, all these tools and techniques encourage boldness and originality, utilizing the intelligence and imagination of the participants. They also encourage all stakeholders affected by a problem network to play an active role in its definition and dissolution. The techniques in this category are by far the most flexible and provide continuous feedback, although decisions might take longer to materialize due to the increased number of stakeholders providing input.

In summary, the strengths of the systems-oriented group tools and techniques, with the exception of the flowchart, are that they:

1. Encourage boldness and originality

2. Utilize the intelligence and imagination of the participants

3. Encourage all stakeholders to play an active role

4. Take into account and actually depend upon group dynamics

5. Encourage flexibility in terms of the problem network addressed

6. Maintain interest over the course of the exercise

7. Encourage development of an appropriate vehicle for the implementation of solutions as a critical part of the exercise

The one possible weakness of these tools and techniques is that:

- Solutions will take longer to achieve due to the increased number of stakeholders involved and, therefore, might not be considered timely, although they are usually more comprehensive and richer.

TOOLS FOR MEASURING PRODUCTIVITY

The tools and techniques described up to this point fit problems and problem networks in a social system, a technical system, or a joint sociotechnical system. It is left to the user to define the dimensions of the problem. This next set of tools, however, is used solely to address problems of production. It does so by measuring key variables in the processes involved.

Check Sheet

The check sheet is simply a written record of how frequently something happens, whether it is the number of fenders that come off the line dented or the number of potential customers who hang up before a salesperson can get to them. The rest of the tools described in this section can feed off the information collected with a check sheet.

Refer to the case study presented in Chapter 6 for an example of how a team employed the check sheet in Step 3 of its Quality Journey as it was collecting and analyzing data to select an area for improvement.

Statistical Control Chart

The statistical control chart was developed by Walter Shewhart while he was working for AT&T. It is used to measure variations in a process. It takes samples and plots them against the average.

For example, suppose a cereal box is supposed to contain 16 ounces of cereal. Boxes coming off the line are picked randomly and weighed. The statistical control chart includes a horizontal line across the middle to represent 16 ounces as the desired average. A vertical scale at the left or right edge shows variations, for example, 15.7, 15.8, 15.9, 16, 16.1, 16.2, 16.3. Numbers along the upper or lower edge of the paper denote the sample (1, 2, 3, 4, 5, etc.).

A dot representing each individual sample is placed on the grid at the juncture of the sample number and the defined weight. Two other horizontal lines, one above and one below the horizontal desired average line, show upper and lower control limits.

Employees using a statistical control chart watch where the dots fall so that they can adjust the machine accordingly, trying to cause the next dot to land on the desired average line. Clusters of dots above or below the upper or lower control line, or even within the control lines but above or below the desired average line, are easiest to deal with. Randomly distributed dots are more challenging.

Refer to the case study presented in Chapter 6 for an example of how a team constructed control charts to monitor and control its new process.

Histogram

The histogram is a simple tool that is used to show dispersion. It shows a series of bars on a chart to represent categories with, say, $1/4$ inch representing each of the items in each category being measured.

For example, to discover the dispersion of lengths in a process that produces loaves of bread, count the number of loaves coming off the line that measure 10 $6/8$, 10 $7/8$, 11, 11 $1/8$, and 11 $2/8$ inches. Then, represent each category of bread length with a bar made up of $1/4$-inch units. If the bar representing 11 $1/8$-inch-long loaves is three times as long as any other, there is relatively little dispersion.

Pareto Diagram

This tool literally provides a visual representation of the relative size of problems. First, a constant unit of measurement is defined (for example, $1/4$ inch of a bar may be used to represent $10 in cost). Then, using a bar chart, the number of one type or various types of defects is plotted against that measurement.

An example would be an apparel manufacturing operation where every blouse that has to be rejected at the end of the line is estimated to cost the company $10 in terms of waste. Every pair of pants rejected costs $20. If a manager has to decide whether to deal first with the loss resulting from the blouse operation or from the pants operation, a Pareto diagram comparing the total daily cost of rejected blouses to the total daily cost of rejected shirts should help make the choice more obvious.

Scatter Diagram

The scatter diagram is used to show the relationship between two variables. The objective is to discover whether or not a correlation exists. For example, to find out if college students are absent most frequently from early morning classes, you could develop a diagram with a horizontal and vertical axis. Place the hours classes begin (8:00, 9:00, 10:00, 11:00, etc.) along one axis. Place the number of absences (1, 2, 3, 4, etc.) along the other. Pick an equal number of classes which begin at each hour, controlling for other variables if possible, and then enter a point on the chart for each day that each class meets to show how many students were absent.

If the daily points are clustered at the 8:00/high number of absences intersection, a correlation probably exists. If they are scattered equally over the diagram, however, chances are that no correlation exists between absences and early classes.

One use of the scatter diagram is to verify the relationship between a cause and an effect, similar to the fishbone diagram. Refer to the case study presented in Chapter 6 for an example of how a team used this quality control tool to accomplish this task in Step 8 of its Quality Journey.

Due to the straightforward and totally focused nature of these tools for measuring productivity, it is not necessary to evaluate them.

PUTTING IT ALL TOGETHER

At this point, we have identified those characteristics an organizational culture should have in order to make it conducive to effective problem solving. We have identified team vehicles that will adequately facilitate the efforts involved. Finally, we have identified the tools and techniques that can be used in the problem-solving process itself and have discussed their strengths and weaknesses as well as their relative effectiveness in a wide range of situations.

Now it is time to put it all together, to show how these pieces can and have been combined in a real-life situation. This will be the challenge addressed in the next chapter.

4

MAPPING THE RIGHT APPROACH

ON THE RIGHT TRACK WITH JUST A FEW ADJUSTMENTS

A growing number of organizations are adopting the interactive attitude as well as the systems perspective from which it arises. Many are putting the right team vehicle into place. Some are even making sense with their reward systems. These organizations truly empower their employees and truly involve them in designing any changes which will affect them. These companies effectively utilize the expertise of their employees. Unfortunately, however, most of them, while on the right track, still need to fine-tune their approach.

The major weakness in the normal approach lies in its attitude toward training in general and training in problem-solving skills in particular.

There are two types of training in any normal work situation. The first is the training one must receive in order to meet job responsibilities. This might include training in what information to give customers, what buttons to push to make the machine run, what cabinet to put a specific file in, how to run a maintenance check, or what form to fill out in a specific situation.

Employees are supposed to receive this kind of training immediately after being hired. They also are supposed to receive it when any change occurs—when a new type of account is brought in, a new technology is introduced, when a promotion is received, or when the employee is shifted to another function.

The second type of training concerns what to do when a system or segment of a system that the employee interacts with stops working, is not working as well as it should, or might work better if redesigned. While the first type of training focuses on getting employees ready to do what is necessary, the second type focuses on preparing them to help improve products, production processes, management systems, the work environment, and so on.

It is this second type of training that involves the problem-solving techniques and tools discussed in Chapter 3. However, this second type of training sometimes delivers the wrong skills, can be overdone, and frequently suffers from inappropriate timing.

This is not to say that training is not important to problem-solving and improvement efforts. Not only is it important, it is critical. Yet it is not the *only* critical part that has to be done right, and it should not be the initial concern of organizers. The traditional focus on training as a necessary first step, in fact, is one of the major reasons so many problem-solving and improvement efforts that start out with promise and enthusiasm end up producing very little of the desired positive change.

In order to explore the validity of the above statement, we must first ask why it has been assumed until now by a vast majority of those given responsibility for orchestrating problem-solving and improvement activities in organizations that the formal training of participants must precede all else. Why are the early sessions of so many problem-solving efforts devoted to teaching participants the techniques they will be using? Why are the early months of so many large-scale improvement efforts almost invariably spent sending to classrooms or training retreats great numbers of team leaders, facilitators, and/or middle managers who, in turn, are supposed to teach the techniques they learn to the work force?

Several definable reasons exist for this approach. First, as noted, training is obviously a critical ingredient of the cultural change necessary if the quality of the product or service offered, as well as that of manufacturing processes, management systems, and the work environment, is going to improve. The problem, again, is that we have confused the two types of training—that which allows us to meet job responsibilities and that which focuses on solving problems and making improvements.

The first must necessarily be formalized. Everyone needs it. Specific things must be included. Such training offers a well-defined set of skills which everyone must learn. A lot of it, therefore, can be presented in the classroom.

The catch is that while the skills needed during this first type of training can be spelled out with a high degree of exactitude, those required for the second cannot. Therefore, when the second type of training is being offered in the classroom, the "teacher" might actually be teaching the wrong thing.

The best approach to solving a problem or to making an improvement cannot usually be defined ahead of time. It cannot be spelled out until the problem or improvement itself and the unique characteristics involved have actually been identified. This usually happens in the trenches, where the perspective and atmosphere are very different.

Some trainers react to this realization with overkill. They pile on technique after technique during classes or seminars and hope that students will leave with the necessary arsenal. To the contrary, however, the most frequent result of this tactic is that students leave the class and do not remember much of anything that has been taught.

Other consultants react by ignoring the reality of the situation and attempting to pound into the heads of their students the one technique which they claim fits all situations That one technique, of course, does not fit all situations, and once students get back out into the workplace, they waste a lot of time and grow rapidly frustrated trying to create a marriage between a problem and a technique that enjoy little synergy.

A second reason up-front classroom training is preferred has to do with time constraints. In-house trainers usually have a very busy schedule. They have one or two days to deliver their package at each facility. Hanging around for an extended period of time is not part of their responsibility. Their job is to spread the word as widely as possible. They are judged at least partially by the number of bases covered and/or the number of employees "educated." They are not judged by the effectiveness of the results of what they teach in terms of the bottom line.

Finally, consultants brought in to train have an additional constraint—cost effectiveness. Consultants can ask for more money when training or presenting to a large group in a seminar setting than when spending an extended period of time helping individual teams work through problems or shape improvements.

THE BEST MODEL FROM A MACRO PERSPECTIVE

When we shift our perspective from individuals and teams to the macro picture, the traditional up-front approach to training does not work well either. Such efforts are usually top-down. As a result, by the time that all the required and desired sessions have been completed with staff on all levels and employees are finally turned loose to solve problems or to make improvements, enthusiasm has waned (if it has been generated at all).

At the same time, because it is top-down, traditional training in problem-solving techniques/tools tends to get lost among the many other types of training mandated by upper-level management—zero defects program training, safety program training, technical expertise training, training in cost-cutting techniques, preventative maintenance training, etc.

Also, the traditional top-down approach to training in problem-solving techniques may not always generate the desired commitment to improvement. If fact, it often can have the reverse effect. What it can say to some employees is:

> Because management thinks you can't figure out how to identify problems and make improvements in the systems you've been working with for the last 20 years, we've brought in experts to teach you the necessary skills. The results of this training are going to be amazing. With the new skills we're going to teach you, we believe that you will suddenly be able to identify all those problems that have been lying around for all these years without your noticing them. Not only that, but we believe that you are actually going to be able to help us solve them.

As an example of such managerial shortsightedness, consider the true story of a paper mill where the sheet of pulp/paper being run along the webbing of one of the large paper-making machines kept tearing. This cost the company a lot of money because the machine had to be shut down for 20 minutes to an hour while the sheet was patched.

No one could figure out why the sheet kept tearing. Experts were brought in from corporate. Consultants were hired. Every inch of the webbing was examined. The pulp mixture was tested and experimented with. But the tears continued.

One day, while the mill manager was standing by the machine watching it run, an old-time employee happened to walk by. The manager said, "Jess, I don't get it. We've tried everything, but this sheet just keeps tearing."

Jess hesitated a long while, then shook his head and said quietly, "You haven't been looking at the right thing."

The manager glanced sharply at him and said, "What are you talking about, Jess?"

Jess pointed and replied, "See that window up there on the wall above the machine? When it gets really hot in here, people open it to help cool things down a bit. When the breeze is coming from the southwest, it blows directly through that window and tears the sheet."

The manager's response was, "Jess, we've been working on this for six months. Why didn't you say something?"

And Jess replied, "I didn't want to get into trouble. I'm not supposed to think about things like that. I haven't been trained to think about them."

The key is that most workplace problems could be solved more rapidly and comprehensively if managers simply asked the employees dealing with the system involved for their input, listened carefully and sincerely to the response, and then asked the employees to help make the necessary correction.

Employees know what the problems are in their areas of expertise better than anyone else. They also frequently know the solutions to the problems. What organizations need is the culture, the attitude, the perspective, the vehicle, and the type of training which will allow management to take advantage of the employees' knowledge and their ability to make improvements.

With this objective in mind, an alternative to making formal process-related training the initial and primary focus of problem-solving and improvement efforts is to make it part of more results-oriented activities. The most important objective of organizers, if this alternative is adopted, is to very quickly get employees directly involved in improvement efforts. It is to quickly begin generating highly visible results based on employee expertise in both the production process and the work environment.

Training, in this scenario, is delivered on an as-needed basis. Team facilitators are trained on the job as consultants bring the first teams up. Further process-related training needs are identified and frequently designed/met by the team members themselves.

INTO THE TRENCHES

The following case study is presented in order to further explore the strengths of action-oriented training in problem solving. The organization was the Louisiana Mill of the International Paper Company, the site of our earlier example. The effort took place in the late 1980s. No training was given to the top-level managers. They were simply told what was going to happen so that when it did happen, it would be less threatening.

The next step was for the mill manager to identify a head facilitator. That person would work closely with the consultants. The consultants would be responsible for teaching the head facilitator everything they could about team building and problem solving. The objective was for the head facilitator to take over the process as quickly as possible.

The new head facilitator then identified a group of team facilitators. Neither the head facilitator nor the team facilitators, once identified, were given up-front, formal, classroom-based training.

The mill manager, together with his direct reports, was then asked to break the organization chart down according to function so that a network of problem-solving teams could be created. This was relatively easy to do. The work in a paper mill has definite, well-defined stages. At least one team was formed to represent each of these stages.

Within three weeks of the initial discussions with the mill manager, the action part of the approach, coupled with on-the-job training, commenced. The consultants started bringing up hourly teams using the breaking the ice technique. Team members were not taught the technique, but were simply led through it.

The on-the-job action-oriented training for the head facilitator began with that person watching a consultant working with the first problem-solving team. The head facilitator then assisted in working with the second team and eventually took the lead in working with the third or fourth teams, with the consultant observing, supporting, and critiquing afterward.

This same approach was used to teach the facilitators how to run team meetings. The consultant or head facilitator would run the first few meetings and then turn the team over to the facilitator and observe.

Eventually, the facilitators in the network took over the entire team-building and team management process. The consultants, at this point, began to function mainly as troubleshooters and resources.

In this way, teams were defining projects and producing positive results within three to four weeks of their start. Also, at least some of the required training was being completed, but in a more positive manner in that it was "reality" rather than classroom oriented. The facilitators were learning their trade by participating in an actual exercise that produced actual results, actual problematic challenges, and actual commitment, rather than by sitting in a classroom having the steps explained to them and going through mock drills.

The only training that team members had received thus far was again on the job and consisted of being guided through a simple, common-sense approach to problem solving. This approach included the steps of problem identification and exploration, alternative solution development and analysis, cost–benefit analysis of the preferred solution when relevant, and action step definition. Formal training of any type, in fact, was offered only when the team members defined a need for it themselves. At the Louisiana Mill, such requests came relatively quickly, but almost without exception they were for training in skills necessary to meet their normal job responsibilities rather than for process-related skills.

The only people who did eventually request additional training in process-related skills were the facilitators. As the in-house people took increasing control of the team network, they began to realize that in order to keep it productive, they needed ways to stimulate more ideas. At this point, additional techniques were introduced, depending upon the situation. For example, a lot of problem-solving exercises started with brainstorming in one form or another. Again, if a management system problem had a large political dimension, force field analysis might be used.

The facilitators had their own monthly meetings at which they discussed process issues and the projects teams were working on. If a facilitator's team was bogging down in a project, or was losing interest, or had come up with a problem it did not know how to address, various techniques were offered by the consultants to see which would best "fit" the situation. The facilitators then carried these back to their team meetings and introduced them.

Once the teams had enjoyed a number of successes on smaller projects and had developed a sense of ownership, facilitators were also offered the tools for measuring productivity. These tools were introduced to the teams on an as-needed basis. A team might come up with a project where one of the tools, say a check sheet, a statistical control chart, or a scatter diagram, might be of use. At this point, the facilitator would introduce the tool as an alternative or as an aid to achieving a solution. The team would then decide whether or not to use it.

CORPORATE-WIDE VERSUS INDIVIDUAL FACILITY

One might argue that more formal process-related training is necessary when starting a problem-solving effort at the top of a corporation, rather than somewhere down amongst its units. In this instance, the CEO is not the only one who has the power to block or support the necessary changes; a line of vice presidents, division managers, and so on can also affect this process. It is necessary, therefore, to develop the same level of understanding and acceptance in all of these people that was developed up front in the CEO.

More than likely, however, such an approach to training would again not work. The weaknesses of traditional top-down efforts have previously been discussed. These weaknesses include excessive time commitment, lack of understanding, and lack of ownership.

A more acceptable alternative when an entire corporation is involved would be to familiarize the CEO and maybe a few key reports, gain their tentative support, and then immediately drop down several layers, pick a facility, and get the approach at least partially in place. Consultants would begin building the team network at, say, a production facility or in the human resources department several months before beginning full-scale corporate executive-level familiarization.

This staggered approach would prove beneficial in many ways. For one, executive-level familiarizers would be able to say: "Don't just listen. See for yourselves. This is what we are talking about. This is how it works." By this time, a good number of improvement teams at the facility or department would be involved in projects, and several would have produced results. The facility or department, therefore, would provide a "living laboratory" to complement the information consultants were delivering to upper-level managers at the corporate level.

Another benefit would be that once the necessary top-level managers had developed the necessary degree of understanding and commitment, the pilot site could function as a showplace. Staff from other facilities and departments could visit and learn from the pilot site during their familiarization phase.

Finally, one last obvious benefit would be that facilitators from the pilot site would be able to function as consultants at new sites across the corporation, helping to train their counterparts at these sites on the job.

AND THAT'S IT!

Problem solving is a major part of our everyday lives. We solve problems continually as individuals, both at home and at work. Common sense and experience are our two best allies. On occasion, however, a variety of techniques can help us to broaden our perspective in order to come up with new alternatives and better solutions.

Group problem-solving situations are more complicated because more than one perspective is involved. The best solution for one participant in such an effort might not be the best for all. Techniques are needed, therefore, which help us to understand what others are thinking and saying and which encourage the integration of individual perspectives into a far richer group perspective. Finally, techniques are needed to help generate the necessary degree of group-wide commitment to the final solution.

When we reach the organizational level, we must deal not only with individual and group perspectives, but also with those of organization segments and the organization as a whole. Effective problem solving at the organizational level becomes a very complex matter. A lot of time, energy, and money can be wasted by setting up problem-solving efforts and carrying them out in the wrong way.

In order to succeed at the organizational level, we ultimately need a culture (especially a reward system) that encourages participation in and commitment to the processes involved. We need the right attitude and perspective. We need a vehicle which allows the most effective utilization of employee expertise. We need an accurate understanding of the value of the various techniques and tools at our disposal. Finally, we need to know how best to fit all these pieces together into a systemic whole which will allow us to achieve the desired results.

This last need requires an organization-wide process model. One such model, which has been used successfully, will be presented in Chapter 5.

5

OVERVIEW OF THE QUALITY JOURNEY PROBLEM-SOLVING PROCESS MODEL

INTRODUCTION

The Quality Journey Problem-Solving Process is a ten-step model that can be used to diagram and solve any type of problem or opportunity that requires more than a superficial analysis and documentation to effectively reach the optimum solution. The steps in this process are sequential in nature, although some steps may be omitted or replaced as needed. The suggested ten steps are as follows:

1. Create the charter

2. Survey the customers and stakeholders

3. Select the issue

4. Diagram the process

5. Establish the process performance measures

6.   Diagram the causes and effects

7.   Collect data on causes

8.   Analyze data

9.   Develop and test possible solutions

10.   Standardize the process

These ten steps can be grouped into six macro categories as follows:

- The problem

- The process

- The causes

- The numbers

- The solution

- The future

An overview of the interrelations between the various categories and steps, along with a snapshot of the various quality and statistical tools used during the problem-solving process is provided in Figure 6.3 (in the case study).

UNDERSTANDING THE PROBLEM

In many cases, people often start improvement activities without first understanding why the problem in question is being addressed. Often, people become uncomfortable and wonder whether or not the real or correct problem is being addressed or whether there will be a more important issue to work on right around the corner. Problem areas become much clearer when the actual circumstances are compared to the business objective, the process requirements, or the customer expectations. The bottom line is that problem areas must be "discovered."

Two steps are included in this category: (1) create the charter and (2) survey the customers and stakeholders. It is important to set priorities among problems to work on, choosing the ones that appear to be most significant in terms of the following categories: quality, volume, delivery, and cost (as shown in Figure 6.2). Problems are hidden yet they exist all around us, like low-hanging fruit waiting to be picked. Problem-solving activities begin with understanding the facts, organizing the data, and exposing them through data analysis.

STEP 1: CREATE THE CHARTER

> **charter** (char'ter) n. *Abbr. char.* a written grant or document conferring certain rights and privileges to a local branch, chapter or group and which outlines principles, organization and function of the group.

The identification and documentation of the team charter is the critical first step in the problem-solving process. Ironically, it is also the least understood and most frequently omitted or short-circuited. The nucleus of the charter revolves around the establishment of a performance promise that the team can consistently deliver in order to ensure success. According to Bob Lynch of QualTeam, flawless delivery on the performance promise to customers and stakeholders depends upon seamless execution internally. Seamless execution is the result of strong links between internal customers and suppliers. The charter enables every team to consider its role in helping to accomplish the greater purpose of the organization by considering these relationships.

The charter can be viewed as a chain of objectives, which begins with a statement of the mission of the team, followed by the supporting purposes. The length of the mission statement should be between 25 to 50 words. The mission statement describes the core purpose of being for the team. The next section covers team organization and the reporting structure, followed by team member responsibilities. This is followed by the procedures for each of the team's supporting purposes, as well as those items that are out of the scope of the team. Rounding out the charter are the team goals to be accomplished. The following are the key items typically covered within the framework of the charter:

1. Team mission and objectives

2. Products, services, and/or information provided

3. Synopsis of team processes, customers, and their valid requirements

4. Competitive benchmarks, if known

5. Supplier requirements, if available

STEP 2: SURVEY THE CUSTOMERS AND STAKEHOLDERS

The key point in this step is for the members to put themselves (as a team) in the shoes of the customer and develop simple surveys to help identify areas to focus the team on. Some of the areas to cover are:

- Quality

- Speed/timeliness

- Cost and functionality

- Availability and flexibility

- Responsiveness

- Durability

- Reliability

The main goal is to become a high-value organization, and becoming one depends upon the rate of improvement. Customer data and statistics help speed up learning, which is the central purpose of information—to speed up learning, which speeds up improvement. Without change there is no improvement; however, change requires new knowledge and new knowledge requires learning. Thus, rapid improvement using structured problem-solving techniques is all about rapid learning. The "organization" should also be surveyed at this time in order to uncover significant information concerning the areas of quality, volume, and cost.

STEP 3: SELECT THE ISSUE

The selection step of the continuous improvement problem-solving process provides the team with its instrument panel to measure how closely actual performance matches the performance promise. The data that the team uses to evaluate and select the issue to work on must come from the team's processes and customer surveys. This is called the "voice of the organization" and the "voice of the customer."

According to JUSE, selecting the issue or theme for problem solving can be enhanced by the following requirements:

- The theme is directly tied to the worker's personal area of authority

- The problem or issue urgently requires resolution

- Superiors are interested in the issue

- The worker is able to employ his or her own opinions in the problem solving and is able to make decisions

- An evaluation of the project can be made in terms of financial effects, the expected benefits are positive, and it appears that the employee will be able to take pride in the results

- The proposed theme is in line with the long-term strategic plan or the yearly plan

- Dramatic results are expected from the improvement activity

- The time period potentially required by the project is appropriate

The statement of issue or theme should be written in paragraph format and should include a description of why the particular issue was selected.

STEP 4: DEFINE AND DIAGRAM
THE PROCESS IN ORDER TO
UNDERSTAND CURRENT CIRCUMSTANCES

This step involves creating a support or promotion group (if one is not already in place) in order to get started, followed by creating the activity plan and completing the diagram and flowchart of the initial documentation package. The promotion group is usually in the form of a team or an employee-involvement group interested in a certain problem area. If the scope of the activity is very broad, the project can be broken down into smaller components and spinoff teams can be created at this time.

A "communication" team or even a "quality assurance" team may be part of the problem-solving activities.

Once the theme is selected and the promotion group has been formed, the next activity involves building a project rollout plan of activities and key milestones. The plan should be constructed around the management cycle, starting with the vision.

> **Management cycle** = vision, strategy, planning, organizing
> and implementing, controlling

Once the plan has been developed, the following activities should be performed as part of the diagramming and flowcharting activity:

1. Develop a statement that explains the overall purpose of the business process:

   ■ Prepare a one-sentence draft that describes why the process exists.

   ■ Verify that the statement incorporates language that covers cost, schedule, and performance, such as reliability, timeliness, etc.

   ■ Check to see that the statement is one that the business partner(s) would endorse.

2. Define the valid process scope:

   ■ Identify where the process starts or begins (the first activity in the process).

   ■ Identify where the process ends (the last activity in the process).

   ■ Identify all major activities within the process.

   ■ Identify the key inputs that are required from outside the process and the suppliers that provide them.

   ■ Identify the key outputs from the process and the business partners/customers who receive them.

   ■ Identify those major activities and processes that depend upon this process or upon which this process depends for support or input.

   ■ Check the process scope to ensure that it takes into account known significant problems/opportunities for improvement.

3. Identify the key activities that occur in the process and the position or person who performs them and their related inputs and outputs:

   - List all the positions or players in the process and the activities by name.

   - Identify the various inputs that are needed for each activity and the suppliers that provide each input. Group activities where possible.

   - Identify each output from the activity groupings and the customer/business partner who normally receives the output.

   - Identify those activities where there is a need to verify/check/ inspect the output in order to effectively complete the next activity without delay or modification.

   - When the output does not meet requirements, identify the activities that need to be performed instead of, or in addition to, the normal next activity. Identify the position/person who performs these activities when the output does not meet requirements.

   - Identify all additional inputs required for these additional activities, as well as the suppliers that provide the inputs.

   - Estimate the frequency of occurrence of these nonconforming situations.

4. Create a process map or flowchart, based upon the information outlined above:

   - Number the activities identified in Step 3 according to the sequence in which they normally occur.

   - Using a block, square, circle, or other symbol on the flowchart, enter the name of each activity identified and the position/ person who performs it.

   - Map out the process, generally starting at the left and proceeding downward and/or to the right.

   - For those activities identified as needing a check or inspection, create a decision block following the activity block that indicates whether or not the next normal activity can be performed without delay or modification.

- Enter the name of each additional activity identified above in a series of blocks, thus creating a secondary process path. Connect the last block and resume the normal flow.

- Estimate both the elapsed time and the applied time that it takes to complete each activity. Post the numbers above or next to the corresponding block or symbol.

- Use off-page connectors to continue the flow where necessary.

5. If the flowchart becomes too detailed, modify the scope of the process defined in Step 3 and create a summary, higher level macro flow.

6. Additional usefulness can be derived from the flowchart by labeling and grouping activities into "value-added" and "nonvalue-added."

STEP 5: ESTABLISH THE PROCESS PERFORMANCE MEASURES AND TARGETS

In order to develop process measures, it is necessary to identify (1) categories of measure, (2) units of measure, and (3) levels of measurement, as outlined in the following five items:

1. **Categories of measure** identify "what to measure" in a process. Cost, schedule, and performance quality are three such categories. Other relevant categories include quantity, timely use of resources, and leadership. These basic categories of measure should be broken down into more specific levels of customer requirements, using a scorecard matrix as a tool (see Figure 6.2 in the case study for details). David Garvin, in his *Harvard Business Review* article entitled "Competing on the Eight Dimensions of Quality," suggests the following customer requirements as part of the quality categories of measure:

   - Performance—The primary operating characteristics of the product

   - Features—The "bells and whistles" that supplement the basic function

- Reliability—The probability of a product malfunctioning

- Conformance—The degree to which a product's design meets standards

- Durability—The life of the product in terms of economic and technical dimensions

- Serviceability—The speed, courtesy, competence, and ease of repair

- Aesthetics—How a product looks, feels, sounds, tastes, or smells

- Perceived quality—Inferences about quality reputation based on images, models, advertising, or brand

2. **Units of measure** identify the "how to" measure. The units of measure are ratios, ratings, and absolute numbers.

   - **Ratios**—Indicate the percent or rate. Examples of ratios include percent of on-time performance, percent of desired applicants hired, percent turnover, percent system availability (or unavailability), percent rework, percent of process goals met, percent above or below budget, percent overtime, etc.

   - **Ratings**—Indicate satisfaction or perception. Customer ratings are usually along a numerical scale. As shown in Figure 6.2, dimensions of quality are listed and the customer is asked to rate the service, products, and persons involved in a process. Each dimension can also be further ranked both on a scale of 1 to 5 and in terms of priority of importance.

   - **Absolute numbers**—Indicate occurrences over time. Examples include number of customer complaints, number of new customers, number of training courses completed, number of programs tested and completed, downtime due to equipment failure, turnaround time, dollars worth of cost savings and value added, etc.

3. **Levels of measurement**—This is the "why" of measurement. There are three levels of process measurement: mission measures, process output measures, and process variable measures.

   - **Mission measures**—The business results that the process directly impacts on a macro level. Mission measures are the indicators of the fundamental accomplishment of the process in relation to the satisfaction of business objectives. If the process team has stated its charter, then mission measures are the quantitative indicators of its success against it. Mission measures include indicators of quality, speed, cost, customer satisfaction, employee satisfaction, revenue, and profitability. Generally speaking, there should be at least one mission measure for each process.

■ **Process output measures**—The indicators of the success or worth of the process outputs. They are used to track the products or services of an operation and they drive mission measures. Examples include number of reports generated, number of programs finished, number of projects meeting deadlines, etc. Examples of process output measures organized by category and unit of measure are provided in Figure 6.2.

■ **Process variable measures**—The measures that indicate the performance of the process itself, before outputs are produced. They are used to maintain and improve quality by tracking the process. Examples include number of calls answered before the third ring, time taken to produce a program design, effort needed to correct errors, etc.

4. Define the measurements that will determine whether and to what extent the requirements defined previously have been satisfied, beginning with those for the process mission, followed by external process outputs.

■ Identify any existing measures that relate to the requirements. Evaluate the existing measures to determine whether or not they meet all the criteria for valid measures. If they do not, modify them or drop them.

■ For all critical requirements for which there is no existing output measure, determine the appropriate type needed: ratio, rating, or absolute numbers.

■ Ensure that the characteristics of valid measures are satisfied in describing these new measures.

5. For internal process measures, ensure that practical measurements for both effectiveness and efficiency are developed as indicators of process performance.

- Identify measures for those activities that must be performed in order to identify process fail points, which are those activities for which there is a need to check/inspect during the process flow.

- Repeat the steps above to identify measures for all other critical requirements for the outputs/inputs within the process flow.

The next activity involves setting targets. Targets are numeric values that show what level of improvement the activities must achieve. Their focus is on how things ought to be. However, if targets are set too high, there is danger that the plan will fall apart. It is important to carefully judge the current level of progress and the ability to improve in order to set targets at attainable levels that provide sufficient stretch.

STEP 6: DIAGRAM THE CAUSES AND EFFECTS

A flowchart, coupled with other diagramming tools and techniques, can be used to perform this step. The Quality Journal is a diagramming tool which can be used for this purpose (see the discussion of the storyboard technique in Chapter 3 for additional detail). This documentation approach was developed by Lou Schultz of PMI and is an adaptation of the QC Story, the Japanese discipline for solving problems.

Another effective approach is the Process Function Deployment method developed by Dr. Myron Tribus. It has been used extensively to diagram many different types of processes and work flows. A third approach, used extensively for service organizations, is the Service Blueprinting method developed by Ms. Lynn Shostack, chairman of Joyce International.

Regardless of the specific approach to diagramming selected, Tribus suggests the following set of questions which can be used by management to check for consistency of application and use:

- **Why have you selected these as your key processes to diagram?** The response to this question demonstrates whether or not a subordinate is, in fact, involved in continuous improvement. It also determines whether the subordinate and the leader share consistent views as to priorities. If this is not the case, either the leader's priorities were not clearly stated or the subordinate knows something the leader should know about.

■ **What will constitute excellence when you undertake to improve this process? How did you arrive at your definition?** First, determine if the subordinate is clear about what improvement means. In addition, because asking the customer is the only way to learn about excellence, the leader can determine whether the employee knows who the customer is and is attuned to the customer's needs. Finally, according to Tribus, it will be clear whether the person is merely doing what will suffice or is striving for the best possible performance.

■ **What will you measure as the work of improvement progresses? How will you know, before you get to the end of this effort, whether or not you are really making progress?** The purposes of these questions are (1) to discern the quantitative measures the person will use, (2) to encourage the employee to use quantitative measurement if he or she is not so inclined already, and (3) to allow the leader to help the employee use the abilities of others who can demonstrate the use of the quantitative tools.

■ **How will you keep me informed of your progress?**

STEP 7: COLLECT DATA ON CAUSES

Understanding the current situation does not mean just understanding the state of the process at the present time. It also means being aware of the history and variations over time, as well as the state of control. Accomplishing all this requires looking at data and compiling Pareto charts, histograms, control charts, and other quality tools. It also requires the use of stratification when collecting, organizing, and compiling data. The purpose is to gain an understanding of how bad the problem situation actually is. It is also important to understand changes that have taken place over time and to understand problem areas in detail.

The following items should be performed when collecting data as part of Step 7:

1. Identify the purpose of collecting data, including which specific data are required, how the data will be used, and how the data will be displayed.

2. Identify which data are to be collected and used for analysis.

3. Identify who will collect the data (usually the people closest to the work the data represent). It is important to communicate why the data are being collected.

4. Determine when the data will be collected. If sampling is to be used, specify the time of day, week, month, and shift. All data must be collected in a timely manner. Monthly is usually the longest interval and daily is usually the shortest.

5. Decide how the data will be collected. The use of carefully designed forms or spreadsheets can be helpful. Be sure that they are simple, easy to complete, self-explanatory, and take a minimum of time to complete.

6. Decide how much data will be collected and determine the appropriate sample size. The use of a technical resource or statistician may be needed at this point.

7. Collect the data, tabulate, and display using the quality tools discussed in Chapter 3.

STEP 8: ANALYZE DATA

According to a Japanese saying, if the analysis of data is done properly, then the problem is already half-solved. When people cannot discover appropriate ways to solve a problem, it is almost always because they lack a sufficient understanding of the problem and because the analysis of causes was done poorly. The true multiple causes of the problem must be uncovered and efficient corresponding corrective action must be taken.

When a shotgun approach is used (corrective action taken based on a whim), the effort never yields an effective resolution. The starting point for true problem solving is the level of variability, which is documented through the process of understanding current circumstances. Using variability as a base, it is important to define the relationships between the characteristics (results) and the causes and to seek out the true causes of the variability.

A total of 20 or more quality and statistical methods and tools are used in this step, as summarized in Chapter 3. Of these, the fishbone diagram is by far the most popular and widely used of the seven quality control tools. It is often coupled with the TKJ technique, which is one of the new (planning) quality control tools.

STEP 9: DEVELOP AND TEST POSSIBLE SOLUTIONS

This step consists of three separate activities within the problem-solving model:

1. **Researching the improvement plan or hypothesis**—Once the real causes of the problem are known, the next step is to establish a corrective action plan to eliminate those causes.

   ■ It is important that the corrective action plan be specific. Abstractions will not be useful.

   ■ Use the 5W1H (who, what, where, when, why, and how) checklist to clearly specify who will do what.

   ■ Use an affinity diagram to research the many corrective action plans by breaking down traditional ways of thinking and drawing out new ideas.

   ■ Use a corrective action systematic diagram and its structure tree format to help evaluate the plan.

2. **Planning and executing the improvement plan**—The corrective action plan that was researched and established is now ready for implementation in this activity. Since there is usually more than one item in the corrective action plan, it is necessary to schedule the various items so that the effects of each can be verified. The corrective action systematic diagram is useful for this activity, as discussed in Chapter 3.

3. **Verifying and reviewing the results of improvement activities**—This activity involves evaluating the corrective action to determine whether the strategy was to influence the average values of the outputs of the processes or whether it was to influence the variability. The next step is to determine how much the average was changed or to what extent the variability was reduced.

STEP 10: STANDARDIZE THE PROCESS

Two activities are involved in this step: standardization and establishing full control. In order to ensure that the effects of improvement activities are not just temporary, standardization through documentation is necessary. Standardization is defined as the measures that prevent circumstances from returning to their previous state once improvement activity has been implemented and the results verified. A key part of this step is recurrence prevention, which is implemented to maintain the results and effects of improvement activities that eliminate the true causes of the problem. Examples of standards include technical engineering standards, operational standards, and standards relating to systems and work methods.

Once standardization is in place, a system of full maintenance control is needed to sustain the benefits of improvement over the long haul. Setting up a control system generally requires defining control characteristics, discovering control items, establishing control limits, and defining responses to out-of-control situations. To fully establish control, it is important to establish a system to execute the PDCA (Plan-Do-Check-Act) cycle effectively and in a timely manner.

Chapter 6 will now offer a case study of an organization effort in which the Quality Journey Problem-Solving Process was successfully used, incorporating many of the techniques and tools discussed in Chapter 3 and dealing with many of the issues discussed in other chapters.

INTEGRATED CASE STUDY: JIM'S APPLIANCE WAREHOUSE SAVINGS

THE COMPANY

Jim's Appliance Warehouse Savings, better known as JAWS, was founded in 1973 by Jim "service is my middle name" Peters. Within 10 years, JAWS had stores in 14 Florida cities, from Miami to Tallahassee. JAWS stocked a variety of household appliances, televisions, VCRs, ovens, refrigerators, stoves, microwave ovens, and stereos, plus many accessories. Jim owned 80 percent of JAWS, and his brother, Frank, owned 20 percent. JAWS was able to finance expansion through company profits and a long-term loan agreement with First Biscayne Federal.

JAWS' marketing strategy was to display a large selection of appliances, at discount prices, fortified by a well-trained and knowledgeable sales staff and a strong service department. Jim thought that repair services were so important to JAWS' customers that each of the 14 stores had its own in-house service department. Warranty claims and parts purchasing were coordinated through the central office.

By the end of the 1980s, annual sales averaged $60 million and net profits $3.5 million. The service department averaged an annual loss of $500,000, which Jim considered an acceptable expense because it allowed JAWS to maintain at least a 1 percent gross margin pricing advantage over its competitors.

CHANGING CONDITIONS

JAWS' marketing strategy had worked well for many years, but in 1991 conditions began to change significantly. JAWS was still profitable ($1.8 million on sales of $62 million), but it was obvious that some adjustments needed to be considered.

Among the changing conditions were a string of new competitors, which resulted in frequent price wars. Some competitors even mimicked JAWS' in-house service departments. Also, many television and radio repair outlets were performing repairs on all types of appliances (and even selling some appliances on a limited basis). Manufacturers' warranties permitted repairs to be performed at any authorized service company instead of limiting customers to the stores where they had originally purchased the products. JAWS even had to repair products sold by its competitors, which increased the service department's loss to $725,000.

As a temporary measure, JAWS began increasing its advertising budget and offering higher discounts, which resulted in increased sales but at lower profit margins. Jim Peters knew that it was only a matter of time before this temporary strategy was doomed to fail, because increased sales were accompanied by increases in other expenses, including utility bills, computer processing, advertising, storage, and staff.

Jim was constantly monitoring his company's numbers, from sales to daily door counts to the closing rates of salespeople. Jim used to joke, "Making money is easy. You just increase sales and reduce expenses!" Jim found that he had to make both events occur and that wasn't so easy. Reducing expenses too much would break the very spine of JAWS. Increased sales would also cost money. For every dollar of added expense, sales had to increase by seven dollars. By year-end 1992, Jim was no longer joking. If expenses remained the same and the store managers' sales forecasts were on target for 1993, JAWS would barely break even. Jim wasn't sure how he would explain this to First Biscayne, which could pull the plug on JAWS overnight if it felt "insecure," as the loan agreement was worded.

QUALITY COMES TO JAWS

Frank Peters, Jim's younger brother, approached Jim about some articles he had recently read describing how other companies had improved customer satisfaction while increasing productivity. Frank said the concept was fairly simple—find out what is most important to customers and give it to them. Frank was still a little vague on the subject, but he told Jim that JAWS needed to create some structures, develop a long-range "game plan" designed to meet customers' needs, involve the people at JAWS who did the work, and train them in the use of quality tools.

Jim was a little skeptical about Frank's ideas. Hadn't JAWS always been oriented toward its customers? Didn't JAWS have an annual strategic plan, with defined objectives for each store? Weren't employees free to volunteer ideas through the suggestion program? As for structure, it was clear who was in charge, wasn't it? Besides, Frank's ideas (which included a lot of training) would cost plenty, at a time when JAWS was watching every cent!

Discussions about Frank's ideas continued for several months without resolution. Frank finally engaged a consulting company to create a proposal for the training and to do a preliminary survey and analysis of JAWS. Their report caused Jim's blood pressure to rise several points, because it suggested that over 15 percent of JAWS' customers were no longer satisfied in general and over 45 percent were dissatisfied with the service department in particular. The report also noted that there were pockets of discontent among JAWS employees regarding compensation, reduced opportunity to make sales, and having to deal with unhappy customers.

Matters became worse on Tuesday, July 20, 1993 when JAWS' accountant reported that first-half earnings were a negative $175,000! It was probably coincidence, but on the same day, Jim received four extremely critical letters from customers who wanted to return all the merchandise they had bought, citing poor service as the reason.

The next morning, Frank was surprised when Jim asked him about the system he had previously told him about, specifically, how much would it cost to put it into place and how long would it take. Frank suggested they meet with the VRF Group, which had conducted the survey and whose specialty was improving customer satisfaction and performance.

During the meeting, the VRF consultants explained their improvement process and tried to learn the level of Jim's commitment. Persuaded that Jim was committed and would devote sufficient resources, the VRF Group agreed to work with JAWS.

ESTABLISHING A STRATEGY

To begin the implementation program, Joe Martini of the VRF Group conducted a three-day high-level executive workshop, which was attended by Jim and Frank Peters and the other members of the executive committee (Reynold Rubio, vice president–sales; Daniel O'Leary, vice president–finance and treasurer; Norma Vogel, vice president–administration; and Ralph Emerson, vice president–service).

Joe spent most of the first day reviewing the benefits of improving customer satisfaction, involving employees and identifying key measurements and the need for an overall strategy. None of the executives was able to describe JAWS' mission, or reason for being in business, other than it related to "making a lot of money."

There were many questions and much skepticism about the need for a formal mission statement, but Joe was able to persuade most of the group that accomplishing financial objectives could not occur in a vacuum. Those who were not so convinced agreed to keep an open mind. Joe shared the mission statements of various successful companies and suggested that it was time JAWS developed one. However, it would only be meaningful if the leadership of JAWS defined the company's mission. Joe couldn't do it for them.

The next morning's session focused on drafting the mission statement. Suggestions ranged from "being the largest company in the country" to "being the dominant seller of appliances in the state of Florida." In facilitating the workshop, Joe thought the ideas offered were a good start, but they needed to be more specific, more customer oriented, and should include a time frame. On the other hand, a mission statement must be flexible enough to accommodate changes in technology and the marketplace.

Dan O'Leary commented that all of this was very interesting, but as vice president–finance and treasurer, he had to question whether some high-sounding mission was going to pay the bills. "Are we drafting our epitaph?" he asked facetiously.

Joe thanked Dan for raising the issue and promised to connect it later with something to which they could all relate. Joe couldn't help but quote one of Dr. W. Edwards Deming's remarks to the effect that a company without a mission is "...like taking a trip in an automobile by looking out the rear-view mirror. You need to know where you want to go and point in that direction!"

It was an agonizing day, but by dinner time, the executives had developed their first draft of a mission statement, one they all could live with. It read:

> The mission of JAWS is to become within five years (1998) our customers' preferred provider of electronic products and services for their homes in our market areas, providing continually improving value while exceeding their needs and expectations through the active participation of all JAWS employees.

Joe commented that they might want to fine-tune the draft later, but it was an excellent beginning.

To start the third day of the workshop, Joe said that the "...fun was just beginning. Now that they knew where they wanted to go—the mission—they had to decide what was necessary to get there—the strategic objectives—by land or by sea..." Later on, they would need to establish ways to measure their progress toward meeting their objectives.

Joe divided the executives into two groups and asked them to brainstorm lists of what they thought had to be accomplished, on a broad level, to achieve the mission. Later, they would combine the lists and use the affinity process to come up with several key categories. For example, one way to support the mission might be to increase sales levels by providing free delivery or installation of appliances (rather than charging extra for these services, as was JAWS' policy), but these ideas could be grouped under "incentives" or even the broader category of "improve customer satisfaction."

The workshop was extended to four days. The group finally agreed on six strategic objectives which had to occur in order for JAWS to achieve its mission:

- Achieve and maintain 100 percent customer satisfaction with all products and services

- Achieve and maintain 100 percent customer satisfaction with all repairs

- Become and continue to be market share leader in all product and service categories

- Achieve and maintain 100 percent employee satisfaction and involvement

- Achieve and maintain reputation in each community served for high quality and as being responsible corporate citizen

- Achieve and maintain stable financial condition, maximizing shareholder value

One learning experience for everyone was having to function and communicate as a team. For Jim Peters, it meant "leaving his stripes at the door." Through Joe's encouragement, everyone felt free to criticize anyone else's ideas, which was a rather unique concept at JAWS.

Joe said that the next step would be the development of priority or key activities necessary to achieve the strategic objectives. For example, what specific activities were required to achieve 100 percent customer satisfaction? One such key activity might be to create an outstanding management system by developing processes to assure that constant excellence and quality every day were not left to chance. Identifying these key activities would be the subject of the next week's workshop. Joe suggested that the participants might want to discuss these ideas and possible supporting activities with the people in their departments.

Jim Peters issued a memo the next day to all employees, stating the mission statement and the strategic objectives and explaining their significance. Plans were already in the works for Jim and Frank to visit all the stores to communicate the reasons for the changes and to answer questions and concerns. It was critical that employees be kept informed and their fears addressed. While employees may have been fearful of current conditions continuing (flat sales and profits, competitor inroads), they would be just as fearful about the impending changes, even if they knew that the changes were absolutely necessary.

The next week's workshop was very trying for all concerned, but by Friday all the key activities necessary to accomplish the strategic objectives had been identified. The first objective would require successfully accomplishing several key activities, such as improving customer satisfaction with value and pricing and improving effective/caring communications with customers.

For the second objective, the group decided that a few of the same key activities applied, such as improving effective/caring communications with customers. They also added some activities, including reducing the number of missed commitments and providing high-quality repair service.

Next, for each key activity, the group identified one or more indicators to determine how they would measure their performance. For example, to measure progress toward reducing the number of missed commitments, the total number of missed commitments each month would be tracked, distinguishing between missed commitments involving repairs and missed commitments involving sales of products and services. All of the key activities, their indicators, and their related strategic objectives are shown in Figure 6.1.

To determine the indicators for the key activities, lower level measurements would also have to be established, usually on a store-by-store basis. At the end of each measurement period, the lower level indicators would be summarized in a company-wide indicator. This process would require each business unit to track its data accurately and consistently.

Once all the indicators had been established, the next step was to gather the actual data, not an easy task. JAWS already had some of the information in its files, such as sales revenues and expenses, but much of the data did not exist, such as the number of times commitments were missed. It had been three years since the last employee survey, and customers had not been formally surveyed in years. The files were full of various customer comments, most of which were complaints about repair service.

At Joe's urging, Jim and Frank Peters continued to explain to all employees what the new measurement system was attempting to accomplish. Employees might naturally have assumed that with performance being more closely monitored, some heads might roll if the indicators moved in the wrong direction. The Peters brothers tried to emphasize the positive, that no one at JAWS could improve without keeping track of results, like weighing in when on a diet. Despite such encouraging statements, many employees remained unconvinced. Joe hoped that the integrity of the data would not suffer.

Jim Peters was not as worried about the integrity of the data as much as he was concerned about the sheer volume. "Do you realize that to

Strategic Objectives	Priority Activities	Indicators
Achieve and maintain 100% satisfaction for all products and services.	• Develop outstanding quality and delivery system • Improve customer satisfaction with value & pricing • Improve effective/caring communications with customers	– Customer Satisfaction Index (CSI) Summary – Process Indicator Summary – CSI - Pricing component – CSI - Communications component
Achieve and maintain 100% satisfaction on all repairs	• Develop outstanding quality and delivery system • Improve effective/caring communications with customers • Provide high quality repair service • Reduce number of missed commitments	– CSI - Communications component – Process Indicators - Repairs – CSI - Communications component – CSI - Repair component – Total number of missed commitments
Market Share Leader	• Improve development and introduction of innovative products and services • Improve competitiveness	– Percent of sales on new products and services – Customer survey results
Achieve and maintain 100% employee satisfaction and involvement	• Improve employee satisfaction by providing knowledge and experience • Improve communication with employees	– Learning hours per employee – Percent participation on teams – Employee survey results
Achieve and maintain reputation for quality and corporate citizenship	• Develop outstanding quality and delivery system • Encourage employees to participate in community affairs • Reduce number of complaints to Better Business Bureau	– CSI Summary – Percent of employees involved – Total complaints to Better Business Bureau
Achieve and maintain financial objectives, maximizing shareholder value	• Increase revenues • Reduce operating expenses • Increase return on investment	– Total revenues – Total expenses – Net profits + shareholders equity after tax

FIGURE 6.1

know what's going on in my company, I've got to go through zillions of reports and indicators? I guess the days are gone when I could just look at the sales figures and know what was happening!"

Dan O'Leary continued to harp on his favorite theme: even though all these measurements tied to performance and customer satisfaction might be nice to have, nothing was more important than the bottom line. "Try paying the rent with customers' compliments!" was Dan's standard operating phrase.

Joe continued to plead for Dan and the others to be patient. He tried to remind everyone that JAWS was actually remodeling its ten-year-old management system, which had not changed radically from the days when JAWS had one outlet. "You didn't create your existing management structure overnight and you're not going to put a new one in place overnight either. We've got to take things one step at a time and you've got to have faith that JAWS not only will take care of its customers better, but will achieve or surpass its financial objectives."

Joe asked all the executives to read copies of two reports which he distributed, both of which related to a relatively new concept, the balanced scorecard.

THE BALANCED SCORECARD

What Joe asked everyone to read was "The Balanced Scorecard—Measures that Drive Performance," written by Robert S. Kaplan and David P. Norton and published in the *Harvard Business Review*, and "Improving and Measuring Corporate Performance with the Balanced Scorecard," a summary and analysis of many companies' experiences with the scorecard, written and edited by James A. Ryder, Jr.

In the next executive workshop, Joe asked for someone to summarize the essence of the balanced scorecard and why it might be useful at JAWS. To Joe's surprise, Dan O'Leary offered to describe his understanding of the process. Everyone sitting at the horseshoe-shaped table glanced at each other and sat forward in their seats. Dan didn't usually volunteer for presentations.

"I think I see what you've been getting at, Joe," Dan sheepishly admitted. "It appears that the balanced scorecard answers some of our concerns about the measurement system we've been implementing.

"My reading of the process is that we'll be identifying several key categories which are really critical to our success, measuring how well we're doing in each category and balancing them against each other. It means that at the end of the month, we'll look at just a few numbers or indicators within each category to tell us how we're doing. That seems to handle Jim's problem about being inundated with numbers. While the rest of the organization may need to measure performance in some detail, we'll be taking a broader view and having a better handle on where we're going and how well our strategic plans are succeeding, if at all.

"I'm sure all of you remember from the *HBR* article that Kaplan and Norton recommend four key categories, each from a different perspective: customer perspective (how do customers perceive us?), internal business perspective (how are our internal processes performing?), innovation and learning (are we continuing to improve and able to add value to our customers?), and financial perspective (are we satisfying the needs of our stakeholders?).

"As you may recall," Dan chuckled, "I've been a little more than concerned about the last category, the financial perspective. Well, I have to admit that maybe focusing completely on the bottom line could be a mistake. The authors of the two reports make a good case for paying attention to the other categories as well, because they have a heavy impact on the financial category. It'll just be hard living with some lackluster financials and reconciling myself with new records for customer satisfaction."

"Excuse me, Dan," interjected Frank. "I don't think the balanced scorecard concept says that the financial category is last. All the categories are on an equal footing, to be balanced. We shouldn't accept declining customer satisfaction even if accompanied by record earnings either. It just means we look at all four categories and try to manage the business by not improving one category at the expense of the others. Hopefully, we'll find that improving customer satisfaction goes hand in hand with improvements in the other categories. Isn't that how the rest of you view this?" Heads around the table nodded in agreement.

"Well, I guess I went a little too far," admitted Dan. "That's absolutely right. You want to manage your business by reviewing and balancing all the categories. I think what brought me around to believing in the concept was the authors' distinguishing between outputs and output drivers, the items which drive or impact financial success. As a matter of fact, they are saying that financial measures, such as sales, profits, cash flow, return on investment, etc., are important, but by the time you put together your financial reports, those numbers are history. On the other hand, by following the progress of the drivers, such as customer satisfaction, we can act before it's too late.

"The authors have also found that companies which did well in the nonfinancial categories also met their financial objectives, over the long run. Perhaps I have been too focused on the immediate cash flow and the bottom line only because I'm the first person our suppliers call when the bills aren't paid on time.

"Assuming we want to use these four categories, and I think they are an excellent starting point, we need to establish goals within each category and determine the means of measuring progress toward those goals."

"Joe, didn't we just go through this last week when we developed measurements for how well we are meeting our strategic objectives?" an exasperated Jim queried. Everybody looked over to Joe, who was sitting at the side of the room up against the wall.

"Good question," Joe responded automatically. "Yes, we did develop many measurement points, but for different reasons. What we did last week was to figure out how to measure our performance in many of the key activities which must be accomplished well in order to achieve the strategic objectives. That resulted in many, many data collection points. You may recall, Jim, your anxiety about being overwhelmed with numbers. There is no way you could manage JAWS by reviewing those various indicators on a regular basis, from the number of times service commitments were not made to how polite our service reps were to customers, store by store. Indeed, it was never in the equation that you would be studying that data regularly, unless you were focusing on one specific problem.

"Remember, the whole concept of the balanced scorecard is like the gauges on your car's dashboard, to give you a broad picture of the whole situation. Is the oil pressure where it should be? Is the cooling system working? You don't need to know the temperature of the oil or how many gallons are in the radiator, unless you have a problem.

"Fortunately, much of the data we collect for measuring key activities will also be useful for the balanced scorecard assessment. What you'll see each month, however, will be limited to a relatively few numbers in each category, telling you how JAWS is doing. Is customer satisfaction getting better or worse? Are our internal or core processes functioning as they are supposed to? If you need to dig deeper, the data will be there. If that answers your question, Jim, perhaps Dan can wrap up his presentation and we can break for lunch."

"Thanks, Joe," Dan said as he strolled to the front of the room. "Just so we don't think the balanced scorecard is exclusively for executives, let's not forget that the authors emphasize the importance of cascading the scorecard down through the organization. In so many words, this means that individual departments or stores will have their variations of the scorecard, tailored to their units, to the extent they impact the corporate scorecard. In effect, a store manager's scorecard might balance his or her financial performance with the satisfaction of the store's own customers and the performance of the store's critical internal processes. The store may not measure innovation at all, since our research and marketing department has direct responsibility for developing new products and services. Of course, innovation will definitely be part of the corporate scorecard.

"I'm sure you noted some of the lessons learned by the various authors, including keeping the scorecard simple and making sure we consider the human elements in its rollout throughout the company. You know how nervous people are now about the new measurement system. Well, I can see the scorecard as throwing everyone for a further loop, saying in effect that JAWS is putting customer satisfaction ratings on the same footing as the profit and loss. Some of our old-timers will have trouble stomaching this, particularly when their compensation plans are affected by their overall performance. Any more questions?"

Ralph asked, "What was that about compensation?"

Before Dan could answer, Jim took the floor. "You heard right, Ralph. Our thinking is that if we're going to improve in these critical categories, we can't give lip service, saying we want to improve customer satisfaction but your bonus will depend on your meeting your sales or budget objective. Effective next quarter, all incentives and future evaluations will be tied to the scorecard."

Ralph grinned and, referring to his sometimes temperamental Dade service manager, said, "Wait until Hank Bull hears about this!"

The group broke for lunch, where Joe sat with Jim and Frank. Joe admitted that the executives were looking a little overwhelmed, what with developing one set of measurements last week and then having to develop what appeared to be a parallel system, the balanced scorecard. There was no going back now, but perhaps they should have started with the balanced scorecard, developed appropriate measures, and then gradually added measurement points which were not part of the scorecard.

Following the lunch break, Joe thanked Dan for his presentation and summarized the highlights. The group agreed to adopt the four key categories referred to by Kaplan and Norton. Certainly, success in each of these areas was absolutely essential to JAWS' overall success. There was no question that financial results were driven by performance in the other categories. The four categories were

1. Customer perspective

2. Internal business perspective

3. Innovation and learning perspective

4. Financial perspective

The next step in implementing the scorecard would be to set goals within each category and to establish measurements for each goal. For example, under the customer perspective category, JAWS might establish goals relating to product and service quality, delivery or service time, and cost/value of percent of customers' business done with JAWS. If the goal were 100 percent on-time delivery, then that would be measured from the customer's perspective (and not when the product left a JAWS store).

It took two weeks, but the executives finally developed their first balanced scorecard. The managers solicited input from their departmental colleagues, trying to involve them in the process as much as possible. The final scorecard, with the goals and measurements, is displayed in Figure 6.2. Jim quickly distributed a memo to all employees, sharing the scorecard and the methodology behind it.

Once the data were collected and formatted into the balanced scorecard, it did not take long to ascertain where the scorecard was out of balance, or tilted. The executive council knew that the financial situation was headed in the wrong direction. While information about two categories (internal performance and innovation and learning) was still scarce, the customer perspective numbers were available, and they were alarming! If customer satisfaction were a key driver of financial results, Jim and Frank Peters were not going to sleep well any time soon.

The most difficult part of improving customer satisfaction was deciding where to start. Customers seemed unhappy about everything: pricing policies, credit plans, expertise and courtesy of the sales staff, store atmosphere, return policies, repair and service quality, delivery charges, etc. Jim began to wish he had listened a little longer to the Chicago chain that wanted to buy him out two years earlier.

Customer Perspective

Goals	Measures
• Be preferred provider	– Market share – Sales trends – Survey – CSI - Retention component
• Retain existing customers	
• Meet commitments for delivery, service	– Total commitments missed
• Meet customer expectations for repair service	– Total complaints – Total commitments missed
• 100% Customer satisfaction with value/pricing	– CSI - Pricing component

Internal Business Perspective

Goals	Measures
• Increase productivity	– Revenue vs. number of employees
• Develop and maintain outstanding quality and delivery system	– CSI summary – Key process and quality indicators
• Involve employees in improving productivity in satisfying customers	– Percent of employees on teams – Hours of training – Employee survey

Innovation and Learning Perspective

Goals	Measures
• Introduce new products and services to market first	– Percent of sales from new products and services – Total products and services introduced by competitors
• Continue to improve customer satisfaction	– CSI summary

Financial Perspective

Goals	Measures
• Survive	– Cash flow
• Succeed	– Monthly financial statements of revenue and expenses by store and by division/department
• Prosper	– Return on investment

FIGURE 6.2 JAWS' Balanced Business Scorecard

SETTING PRIORITIES

In their next meeting, Joe suggested to Jim and Frank that JAWS could not undo all its bad practices with the snap of a finger. For long-lasting improvement, things had to be thought out and solved once and for all, but that would take time. The only way to proceed while maintaining sanity was to set priorities and attack the biggest problems first, throwing all the company's resources into the fray. Joe was reminded of a Japanese counselor's observation that trying to solve everything at once was like "…chasing too many rabbits. You don't catch any!"

From their surveys and discussions with JAWS' customers and employees, it was clear to Joe and his associates at VRF that the biggest customer satisfaction issue at JAWS was not its pricing policy, but its service department. It was agreed that all efforts should be focused there first. In addition to affecting the customer perspective category on the balanced scorecard, improving customer satisfaction to 100 percent was one of JAWS' priority objectives. Without an effective and efficient service department, that objective was unachievable.

Jim Peters was relieved that the initial efforts would involve only the service department since that would confine much of the initial training expenses to a relatively small portion of the company. While committed, Jim was still watching expenses pretty closely.

IMPLEMENTATION

Because JAWS' service departments were located throughout the state, VRF's strategy was to do all the training for the 14 service managers in Orlando, located in central Florida. They would be introduced to the general concepts of customer satisfaction and, through improvement, shown how productivity could actually be improved. Repair technicians would be trained at four locations, depending upon their proximity. Training for technicians would focus on problem solving and team participation. The service reps, who answered the service phones and recorded customers' problems, would be trained a few months later.

VRF continued to emphasize that Jim and Frank Peters had to demonstrate their total support for the new way of doing things, a focus on customers and employee involvement, and that a successful culture change was as critical as using the new quality improvement methods and tools.

INITIAL TRAINING

Seven technicians from the Dade County (Miami) service department were combined with eight from Broward County and six from Palm Beach County for a week of training in September 1993.

The five-day course included quality tools and techniques (Pareto chart, fishbone diagram, brainstorming, etc.) and an introduction to the ten-step problem-solving methodology, the Quality Journey. The Quality Journey employed a four-by-six-foot storyboard (or storybook) on which each step was represented by a rectangle large enough to display appropriate documentation (see also Chapter 3).

The principal advantages of the storyboard were to provide a structure for teams while solving problems and to serve as a common communication vehicle. The storyboard would be placed in a hallway or other common area for others in the department to view. The Quality Journey ten-step process is shown in Figure 6.3.

Some training participants were skeptical; they wondered if their paychecks, or even their jobs, would be affected if productivity actually increased. A few remarked that this was not the first "great new program" they had heard about. Many were impressed but did not think management would really support their efforts. Ironically, in the training for service managers, the managers were skeptical that the technicians cared enough to get involved in making improvements. One very skeptical manager was Henry "Hank" Bull, the Dade service manager.

DADE SERVICE DEPARTMENT

When they returned to their service benches, the technicians found that their backlogs had doubled in their absence during their week of training; therefore, they did very little during the next ten days in the way of applying their new skills.

When the Dade technicians met for the first time as a team, they agreed to meet once a week (on Wednesdays) for an hour. The team members were Susan Atkins, Roberto Suarez, Ann Jacobson, Tommy Perkins, Irwin Katz, Janet Hawkins, and Chris Ingram. The team decided to call themselves the Electrons. Janet Hawkins was elected team leader. They unanimously agreed to follow the "Rules of the Road," suggested in the training class. The rules required that each person's ideas be re-

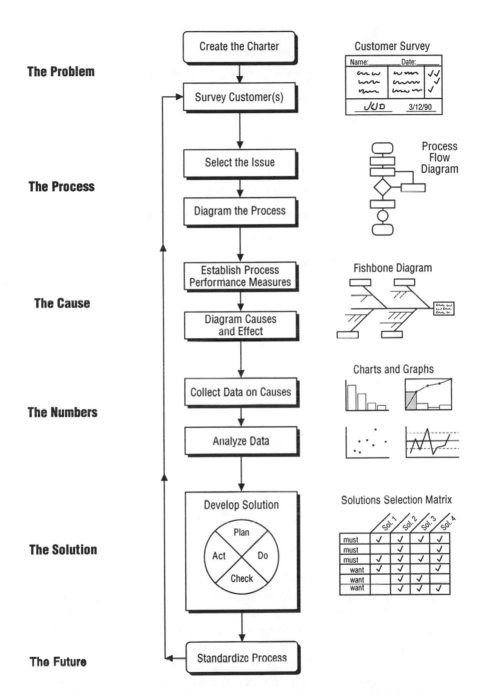

FIGURE 6.3   Ten-Step Storyboard Quality Journey Problem-Solving Process

1. **Attend all meetings on time**

2. **Keep an open mind to the ideas of others**

3. **Avoid interrupting**

4. **Participate**

5. **Speak with facts, avoid subjective opinions**

6. **Respect others**

7. **Give attention to whoever is speaking**

8. **Let everyone have his/her turn to speak**

9. **Suspend certainties**

10. **Share responsibility**

FIGURE 6.4 Rules of the Road

spected, that everyone listen with an open mind, and that everyone was expected to participate. A copy of the "Rules of the Road" poster is displayed in Figure 6.4.

Joe Martini of the VRF consulting firm was designated as the team's facilitator. Teams were formed at the other 13 JAWS locations, but Joe was the only experienced facilitator. The other facilitators were trained in a three-day VRF workshop.

THE TEN-STEP QUALITY JOURNEY BEGINS

Step 1: Create the Charter

Because top management had determined that improving the service department was the number one priority required to achieve 100 percent customer satisfaction, the Electrons' team charter was impacted. A charter states a team's reason for being, or the mission it is seeking to accomplish. During the course of a problem-solving team's activities, it is important that the team does not lose sight of its purpose.

At Joe's suggestion, Janet divided the team into two groups, A and B. Each team was responsible for drafting a charter statement. Group A focused on the technical issues ("improve technicians' skills so that repairs would be done more productively"). The other group had a broader scope ("improve service to all customers, whatever is required").

When the team met as one unit again, everyone acknowledged that a good statement lay somewhere between the two drafts, but they reached an impasse. Some members frequently changed their minds.

Finally, Joe suggested that they identify the attributes of an ideal service department and try to determine the team's potential role in arriving at that ideal state. For each attribute, the team would brainstorm possible alternatives (if answering the phone promptly were a desirable attribute, alternatives might include adding more people to answer phones, a voice mail system to handle overflow calls, etc.). Using this morphological forced connection process, the team would then select various words from the alternative lists and "connect" them in novel ways, perhaps arriving at a good charter statement (see Chapter 3).

This unique exercise created a multitude of new ideas and finally resulted in the following charter statement for the Electrons:

> Our charter is to improve customer satisfaction through identifying key customer concerns about service, specifying the areas where we fail to address such concerns, and taking the responsibility for eliminating such failures systematically, within our service district. We will involve all employees at the company, as appropriate, in order to achieve this objective.

The charter statement was placed in the first rectangle on the four-by-six-foot Quality Journey storyboard. Joe commented that the statement correlated well with the broader concept behind the balanced scorecard.

Step 2: Survey the Customer(s) and Stakeholders

Data were available from several sources to determine customers' concerns and needs. JAWS had an accumulation of letters and other comments about its service; most were negative. Many of the technicians and other service personnel had long-lasting recollections of numerous problems. Most of these data were not organized or compiled, but simply filed in cabinets with service orders.

With Joe's help, the team designed a two-part survey that would be given to each service customer during the next 30 days, beginning November 1. The first part asked customers to rate their concerns regarding service on a scale of 1 to 10, where 10 indicated extremely concerned. A total of 15 items were listed for rating, including the cost of repairs, time to repair, courtesy, etc. The second part of the survey sought customers' opinions about how well JAWS was performing in each of the 15 categories, based on a scale of 1 to 10, where 1 indicated extremely poorly.

The two parts of the survey would tell the team not only what JAWS was doing poorly (and well), but the degree to which such poor (or good) performance mattered to customers.

At Irwin's suggestion, the team agreed to call at random 200 customers who had repairs made in the past 30 days (from 10/1/93 through 10/31/93) and ask them the same questions. The telephone sample would be designated Sample Y and the other survey Sample X.

All the team members participated in the survey. A major problem was the failure of a few service reps (who were not on the Electrons team) to solicit feedback from every customer. After Janet complained, Hank Bull, the service manager, reluctantly ordered the reps to survey all customers. Hank was still a little more than miffed about his bonus package being tied to customer satisfaction rather than productivity, as it was in the past. More surveys were produced, but this alienated some employees (and a few customers who did not want to take the time to answer questions).

Susan, Irwin, and Chris were responsible for compiling and analyzing the survey, which produced the following results:

1. A total of 387 customers were surveyed, 187 in Sample X and 200 in Sample Y (the telephone surveys).

2. The responses from both groups surveyed were virtually identical.

3. Using Pareto charts, Susan, Irwin, and Chris documented the findings. Both samples indicated that the time for repairs was the chief customer concern (68.8 and 70.3 percent, respectively, out of all possible concerns) and that JAWS deserved a "1" for its consistently poor, slow repair times (69.7 and 64.2 percent of all "1s"). The Pareto charts are displayed in Figures 6.4 to 6.8.

4. In the telephone surveys (Sample Y), Irwin said that once it was clear that the time to make repairs was a problem, he and the others began asking customers what they thought was an acceptable time. While 15 percent of those surveyed said that a week was acceptable, 65 percent thought that two working days was the

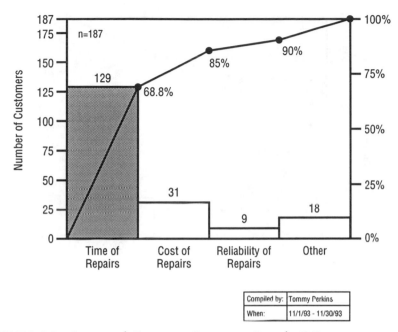

FIGURE 6.5   Survey of Customer Concerns: Sample X Survey

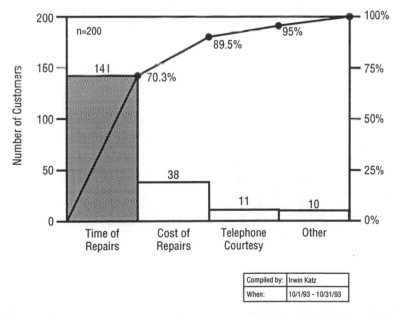

FIGURE 6.6   Survey of Customer Concerns: Sample Y Telephone Survey

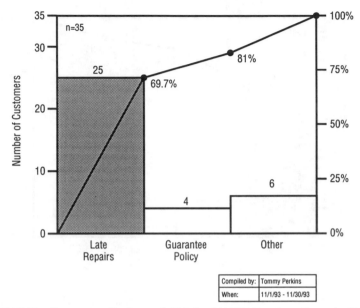

FIGURE 6.7   Customer Ratings of "1" for JAWS' Service: Sample X Survey (35 of 187)

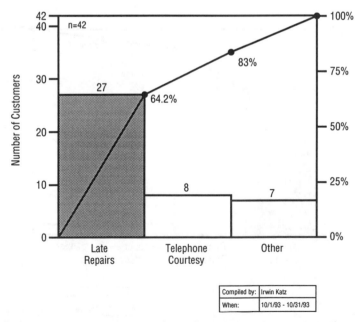

FIGURE 6.8   Customer Ratings of "1" for JAWS' Service: Sample Y Survey (42 of 100)

absolute maximum, and 17 percent indicated one day. Some customers said that the answer depended on the type of product being repaired (i.e., a VCR or refrigerator).

Other team members stated that the "explosion point" for most customers seemed to be about three days, even if they were told in advance that the repair would take longer.

Step 3: Select the Issue

Based on the survey, the Electrons team concluded that the data overwhelmingly indicated that the slowness of repairs (or perceived slowness) was what the team should try to improve. Ann had gathered some additional data, going back to the beginning of 1993, and found that the average JAWS repair time ran between 4 and 6 days and that it was currently about 4.5 days. Obviously, some repairs were taking even longer than that! The team selected average repair times for all appliances as its principal indicator and developed a trend line chart to track the indicator (see Figure 6.9).

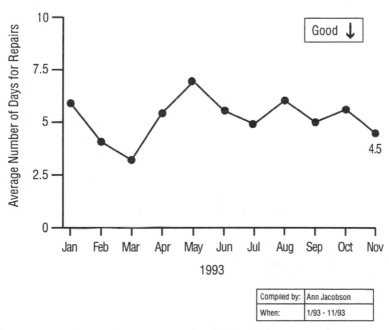

FIGURE 6.9 Average Repair Time for Appliances: Dade County Service Center

Some team members were surprised that the reliability of repairs was ranked third by customers in Survey X, behind both the repair time problem and cost of repair. Roberto questioned whether the survey covered a long enough period, but finally agreed that slow repair time was a major aggravation that needed to be solved.

Tommy suggested that they should also try to improve reliability and cost, the other two customer concerns. Janet reminded the group that the problem-solving process, the Quality Journey, worked best if the team concentrated on fixing one problem at a time. Through communications between the Electrons and the management council, management would be informed of the results of the survey and could create additional teams to address other problem areas.

With the major area for improvement selected, the next question was to decide whether to stratify, or break down, the problem into one issue. Should all slow repair times be lumped together? Could they all be solved in the same way? Were some types of appliance repair times more critical to customers, as the survey indicated? Were late repairs associated with only some technicians? Did some brands take longer to repair? Was the problem seasonal? Did it matter whether customers brought items to the service department or technicians made in-home repairs?

The team began to collect information on a check sheet, one of the seven quality control tools (see Chapter 3). The training class had stressed that as part of the Quality Journey, data needed to be collected, analyzed, and stratified from different perspectives to determine if there was a significant pattern. Instead of looking at all late repairs, maybe certain types accounted for the majority (the Pareto principle or 80–20 rule). One of the pages from the team's check sheet is displayed in Figure 6.10.

According to the Pareto principle, a relatively low number of types of causes (20 percent) may account for a disproportionate number of problems (80 percent). By looking for such disparities, considerable improvement in an overall situation can be achieved by eliminating just one of the causes.

The first few Pareto charts indicated no pattern. It did not seem to matter which technician performed the late repairs, the brand of appliance repaired, or on which day of the week the repair was begun. However, the fifth Pareto chart told a different story. It examined types of products repaired late (417 units taking more than 2 days) during the previous 90 days (9/1/93 through 11/30/93) and indicated that refrigerators accounted for 52 percent compared to 18 percent for VCRs, 9 per-

Date	Day of Week	Type of Product	Brand Name	Over Counter	On-Site	Time to Repair
9/1	Wednesday	VCR	JVC	✓		4 days
9/1	Wednesday	Amplifier	Pioneer	✓		6 days
9/1	Wednesday	CD Player	Kenwood	✓		5 days
9/1	Wednesday	Refrigerator	GE		✓	5 days
9/1	Wednesday	Television	RCA		✓	4 days
9/1	Wednesday	Refrigerator	Amana		✓	6 days
9/1	Wednesday	VCR	Panasonic	✓		3 days
9/7	Tuesday	Refrigerator	GE		✓	5 days
9/7	Tuesday	Speaker	JBL	✓		8 days
9/7	Tuesday	Oven	GE		✓	4 days
9/7	Tuesday	Refrigerator	Kenmore		✓	5 days
9/8	Wednesday	CD Player	JVC	✓		4 days
11/30	Friday	Refrigerator	GE		✓	6 days

Total Repairs: 417

Compiled by: Chris Ingram
Roberto Suarez

FIGURE 6.10   Check Sheet: Late Repairs (From 9/1/93 to 11/30/93)

cent for TVs, and 21 percent for everything else. The average repair time for refrigerators was 6.2 days. The Pareto chart is shown in Figure 6.11.

The team agreed that this was probably true, because refrigerators were always repaired in people's homes by outside service technicians, and it seemed like there were always problems associated with outside service. At one time, JAWS even considered using another company to make outside service calls, but the sales department vetoed the idea.

Susan added that she could not think of a worse situation than taking several days to fix a refrigerator. (During the days and weeks following Hurricane Andrew, the lack of a refrigerator bothered her family even more than the absence of air conditioning.)

Following their problem-solving methodology, the Quality Journey, the team developed a problem statement. They tried to be as specific as possible about the nature of the problem. The statement read:

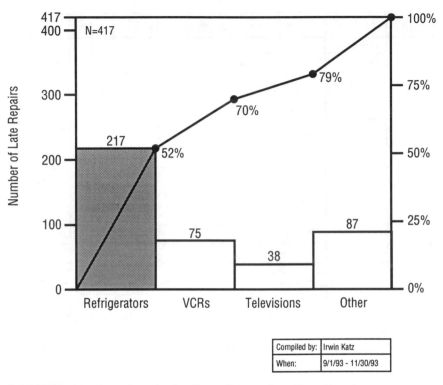

FIGURE 6.11   Late Repairs by Type (More than Two Days)

52 percent of repairs over 2 days involved refrigerator repairs during the 90-day period ending November 30, 1993, in the Dade County service department, failing to meet customer expectations that such repairs take no more than 2 days.

A clear definition of the problem would focus the team's efforts to solve the problem. As Joe remarked, "A problem well-described is half solved!"

The team established repair time for refrigerators as a lower level indicator and selected a target of one day to strive for, although customers might accept two days. Chris wondered if the one-day target was too ambitious because only 18 percent of repaired refrigerators were being repaired within two days, i.e., 82% were taking more than two days (which accounted for the large proportion of refrigerators in overall late repairs).

Step 4: Define and Diagram the Process

After completing Step 3 of their Quality Journey and posting the documentation on the storyboard, the Electrons moved on to the next step—documenting the existing process. How was the JAWS service department repairing refrigerators now?

Although there were service manuals and procedures (from answering the phone to the type of screwdriver to use), there was no comprehensive description of the process to repair refrigerators.

Since the team members worked in the service department, they had the best understanding of the current repair processes, even when those processes did not equate with prescribed procedures.

Following the Quality Journey process, the team began to develop a process flow diagram, or flowchart, to show all the activities that occur from the moment a customer calls about a refrigerator repair until the time the customer is satisfied that the repair has been completed satisfactorily (see Chapter 3).

There are many advantages to using a flowchart. First, a flowchart is a visual representation that shows the linkage of all key activities, something verbal descriptions often fail to achieve. With a flowchart, it is easier to identify critical points, such as when people have to make decisions (which can lead to delays) and when certain activities must be accomplished before other activities, or processes, can begin. Measurement points can be placed on the flowchart to assess whether the process is operating properly and is in control.

Through the exercise of developing a flowchart, a team or individual gains insight into its current process. Team members often identify various "what if" scenarios that may not have occurred to other team members.

Working with Post-Its, the Electrons team brainstormed all of the steps and activities they thought occurred between the time a customer first calls JAWS through completion of the service. One Post-It was used for each activity. The reason for using Post-Its is they allow for flexibility if team members change their minds about the sequence of steps.

Janet suggested that for the time being, they identify the process from a macro or global standpoint (i.e., the "big picture"). Once the process was documented, they would take each major activity and develop micro flowchart steps. For example, in the earlier stages of flowcharting, they would not get into details such as describing what occurs when a customer will not be home at the time JAWS suggests. Rather, the flowchart would succinctly state: "schedule appointment." The macro description might also indicate that the "tech drives to customer's home," rather than several mini-activities, such as "locate map, check gas gauge, etc."

Two meetings were required for the Electrons to develop the macro flowchart and reach consensus that it was a true representation. They identified six key macro activities:

- Customer needs repair

- Service rep takes customer call, writes up service order, makes appointment

- Service tech assigned

- Service tech drives to customer's home

- Service tech makes repair

- Service completed, customer satisfied

Not reflected on the macro chart were everyday occurrences, such as what occurred when no techs were available to be assigned, when the tech could not locate the customer's home, when the repair could not be completed on one visit, or when there was a scheduling problem. The macro flowchart is displayed in Figure 6.12.

The next step was for the team to create a detailed, or micro, flowchart showing these types of everyday occurrences. One difficulty was determining the degree of detail to include so as not to get bogged down. Within micro activities lay sub-micro activities, and there was a tendency to want to include every possible scenario. The team's micro flowchart is shown in Figure 6.13.

The micro flowchart included numerous diamonds, or decision points, that reflected various alternative sequences. As a sanity check, the team had some of the nonteam members review the flowchart to ensure that it was accurate and easily understandable. Hank Bull, the service manager, said that the process flow diagram "looked OK to him."

Joe complimented Janet and the team on their high level of cooperation and their progress up to that point. (Sometimes people in the same department can have major disagreements about how they perform their work, which adds to the time taken to develop such a chart.)

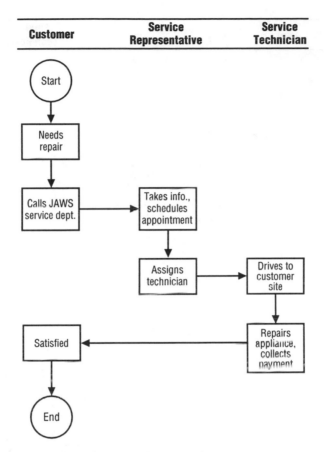

FIGURE 6.12 Macro-Level Flowchart: Dade County Service Department (Process Description of Service Calls for Refrigerator Repair)

Step 5: Establish the Process Performance Measures and Targets

Janet reviewed the Quality Journey storyboard and pointed out that the team was almost to the half-way point in its journey. The storyboard contained all of the documentation for the first four steps. The team then had to decide which points in the process flow diagrams were critical, where measurement points would be established, and those places where data had to be collected and analyzed.

Before proceeding, Joe pointed out that the process of constructing a flowchart was a good example of why a team benefits from following a

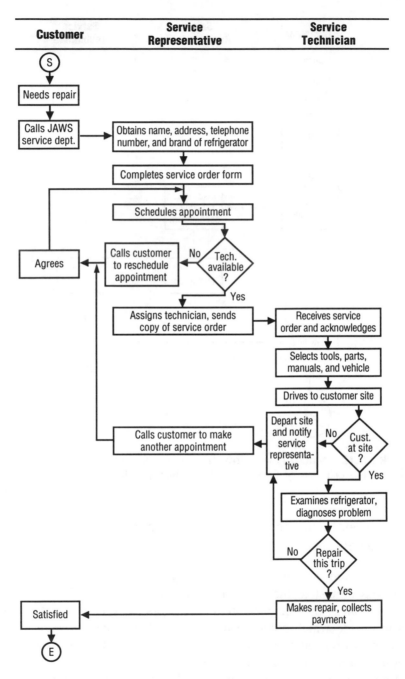

FIGURE 6.13   Micro-Level Flowchart: Dade County Service Department (Process Description of Service Calls for Customer-Site Refrigerator Repair)

structured problem-solving process. Without a flowchart (which shows visually all of the activities involved in making refrigerator repairs), the team would have been only guessing about what to measure. It might have measured the wrong things, which were not necessarily critical to improving repair time. For example, while the number of times the service phone rings before being answered may be important for other reasons, the extra few seconds does not significantly impact the total repair time.

As Janet approached the flowchart (which ran the length of the 17-foot meeting room), Tommy wondered why they needed additional measures. After all, he said, the team knew that refrigerator repairs were averaging 6.2 days (4.5 days for all appliances) and that only 18 percent of repairs were done within 2 days. It was up to the team to improve that number to 100 percent, wasn't it? A few other members looked similarly befuddled. Janet glanced at Joe, a little unsure about what to say next.

Ann, who had taken several quality improvement courses, asked if she could respond. She acknowledged that while Tommy was absolutely right, that their goal was to achieve 100 percent of the target (which was one day, not two days), the total repair time was an outcome indicator or "Q" indicator (for quality). Unfortunately, outcome indicators are necessarily after the fact; they do not provide any information about what is happening before the end result.

What Step 5 is about, Ann stated, is developing meaningful measurements, known as process indicators, that tell more about a process, so the process can be modified it if it is not operating properly. For example, the team might want to measure the time between requests for service and assignment of a tech, or the drive time to customers' homes, or how many times second trips are required because customers are not home.

Obviously, not every point on the flowchart needs to be measured. What the team had to do, Ann summarized, was to select critical points, or milestones. With more data, the team would be on its way to analyzing the causes of late repair times. Once the improvements were implemented and proved successful, these key measurement points would be required to monitor the steps in the process.

At Janet's suggestion, the team began establishing measurement points on the process flow diagram. They agreed to put a Post-It with a large "P" at any point suggested by a team member as long as he or she made it clear what would be measured (days, minutes, number of occurrences or failures) and why it might be important. Once all the process or "P" indicators were posted, the team would evaluate the overall importance of each one. Another factor was the relative difficulty of collecting the measurements.

Irwin suggested that, depending upon their analysis, the team might have to establish further measurement points once they had identified key problem areas.

After four meetings, an exhausted team agreed on the following process measures:

- Number of calls regarding refrigerator repairs
- Number of such calls where time was critical
- Number of calls where customer apparently knew what the problem with the refrigerator was (ice-maker leaking, wouldn't cool enough, wouldn't defrost)
- Number of calls when customer was uncertain about problem ("won't work")
- Time to make assignment to tech
- Number of times no tech was available when needed
- Number of trips per day per tech
- Number of trips to same customer
- Average time of tech trips
- Number of times tech did not drive directly to customer's home (i.e., lost)
- Number of times customer not home, requiring second trip
- Number of refrigerators repaired on first trip
- Number of refrigerators not repaired on first trip
- Number of refrigerators repaired but requiring more trips
- List of categories why repairs not completed on first trip (wrong tools, parts)
- Average time to repair refrigerator
- Number of times customer was mistaken about reason for refrigerator problem
- Number of times tech completed assignment on time, compared to total assignments

While not all team members agreed with these measurements (some members wanted more points), they agreed that these measurements would provide much more information than they had previously. As the Quality Journey proceeded, they thought that they could always develop more, particularly as the search for problem areas intensified. The points were designated by "Ps," as shown in Figure 6.14.

The "Q" indicators, reflecting the output (or end result of the process), are shown at the bottom of the diagram since they measure the success of the repair process from the customer's perspective. The customer is much more interested in having the refrigerator repaired correctly the first time (an outcome) than whether the service rep takes too long to assign a tech.

Collecting the data would be very useful in verifying the team's determination of the root causes and would be the basis for assessing whether improvements were actually made.

Joe signaled to Janet that the measurement points they selected looked good and that the team could consider Step 5 to be completed.

Step 6: Diagram the Causes and Effects

The team was then prepared to analyze the possible causes. Tommy and Susan said that they already had the answer—that outside service techs often had to work on multiple types of appliances and no one should expect them to be qualified to repair everything quickly. Roberto, who was an outside tech, disagreed; he said that the service dispatcher assigned techs in accordance with their experience.

Janet refocused the group on the process and reviewed the cause-and-effect (or fishbone) diagram. The problem statement was inserted into the head of the fish (the "effect"). The team agreed there were several generic categories, or bones, any of which could have caused the late refrigerator repair problem. The generic bones were people (techs, service reps), equipment (test equipment, repair parts, vehicles, refrigerator itself), the environment (bad weather), and methods (procedures, forms, diagnostic process) (see Chapter 3 and Figure 6.15).

The team decided to group these major generic bones into four major ones: people (techs), equipment, environment, and methods. Starting with each major bone, the team brainstormed the possible root causes. It was important to ask "why" enough times to assure that they were not just identifying symptoms. After all, if they fixed only a symptom, the problem would resurface someday. For example, if a tech was identified as the reason the problem occurred, it was important to ask why the tech

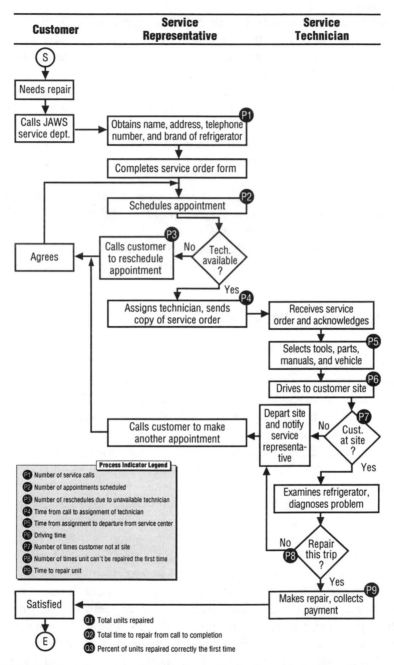

FIGURE 6.14 Micro-Level Flowchart: Dade County Service Department (Process Description of Service Calls for Customer-Site Refrigerator Repair, Including Process (P) and Quality (Q) Indicators)

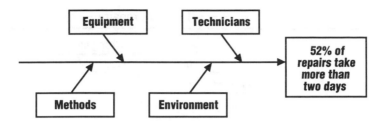

FIGURE 6.15   Cause-and-Effect Analysis: Major Bones

("people") failed to make the repair on time; if the explanation was that the tech had the wrong tools, it was important to determine why he or she had the wrong tools, and so on.

With the first major bone, the team asked "why" several times. There were several bones off the major "tech" bone, including "unable to fix on first trip." Following that path, the team identified several smaller bones, including "wrong tools, wrong parts, can't find repair site, customer not home, unable to diagnose" (see Figure 6.16).

Taking one of the minor bones, "wrong parts," the team went further down that bone and brainstormed several "whys," including "selected wrong parts." The next "why" was "didn't know problem," which in turn might have been caused by "service order incomplete," which may have been the result of "service rep didn't enter enough information on the service order." Why was that? There might be several reasons, including "didn't ask right questions," which could have been caused by "inad-

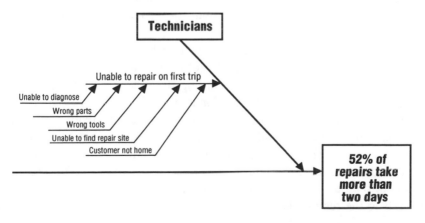

FIGURE 6.16   Cause-and Effect Analysis: Technician Bone

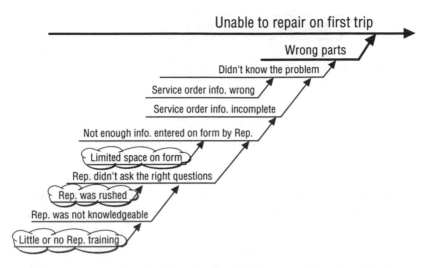

FIGURE 6.17 Cause-and-Effect Analysis: Sub-Part of Technician Bone

equate training of reps" or the fact that reps were frequently rushed because of the company's quota to write up a certain number of calls each hour. A related reason for incomplete information may also have been "limited space on form" (just enough space to write a few descriptive words about the problem). This portion of the tech bone is shown in Figure 6.17.

Tommy suggested that was because the customer did not provide the right information, but Roberto reminded everyone that they were not supposed to ask "why" beyond their area of control. They could control what questions to ask the customer, but they could not control what the customer might volunteer.

Having identified what they believed to be the root causes for the "people" bone, the team highlighted (clouded) the items for emphasis.

The team then asked "why" regarding the other major bones (procedures, equipment, and methods) and found essentially the same root causes, all of which were related to obtaining incomplete information when the customer first called, including wrong tools, test equipment, and even good directions! These root causes were highlighted (clouded) as well.

The team observed that multiple trips to customers' homes were often required to repair refrigerators because the techs brought the wrong tools or parts to the repair sites. In these cases, a second trip would have to be made. This scenario was prolonging the average time for repair, because planning a second trip meant rescheduling with the customer.

Roberto, who made outside service calls, expressed his adamant agreement. Most of the time, he said in an exasperated voice, the only instruction on the service order was that the "refrigerator was broken." The form did not require more information and the service reps did not ask for more details. If the customer's home was a long distance from JAWS' service center, the tech usually could not return the same day, even if the customer could wait. And, Roberto sighed, customers did not understand, because they felt that they had "explained everything that was wrong to the rep!"

With its preliminary analysis of the root cause completed, the team needed to verify its conclusion with hard data by examining the process performance measurements it had been collecting. This verification would take place in Step 7.

Step 7: Collect Data on Causes

The information gathered through the process performance measurements was invaluable. While team members had ample first-hand knowledge of the situation, evidenced by their cause-and-effect diagram, they could not be certain of their conclusion until they looked at the numbers.

Before agreeing to any changes the team recommended, particularly the expenditure of money, management wanted to see supporting data. Since the beginning of the quality effort at JAWS, management was prone to remind everybody to "speak with facts."

Charts were prepared by the team, displaying the number of refrigerators repaired in the 60-day monitoring period (1/1/94 through 2/28/94), separated by on-time and late repairs. Late repairs were segmented by the possible reasons, which included customer not home, not able to make appointment (earlier appointments on the tech's route took longer than planned), electricity off or bad wiring, customer unable to pay, not able to make repair on first trip, unable to locate customer's home, and "other."

Bar charts were also prepared for all refrigerator service orders. The first one compared complete service orders (the ideal state, with all information desirable) with incomplete orders, the latter comprising 91 percent! As Roberto had suggested, many service orders merely stated "refrigerator broken." One set of bar charts is displayed in Figure 6.18.

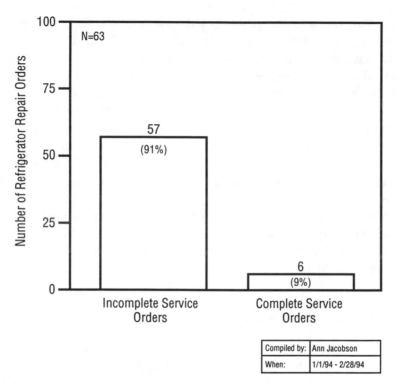

FIGURE 6.18   Refrigerator Service Orders: 60 Days

On another chart, relating to incomplete information, the form was further analyzed. In addition to the cryptic "refrigerator broken," other omitted information included the refrigerator brand, the model, the year manufactured, and comments which might be useful in a preliminary diagnosis, such as whether both the freezer and refrigerator were inoperable or whether the problem was limited to the ice-maker or water dispenser.

Step 8: Analyze Data

Ann suggested that the team employ a scatter diagram, a quality control tool, to plot the relationship between incomplete information regarding the problem description and the late repairs, to see if a correlation existed (see Chapter 3).

Data were grouped according to the length of time for the repair and the amount of incomplete information as a percentage. If the team's assessment was correct, there would be a high correlation between the two types of data.

The paired data (88 percent, 3 days; 67 percent, 4 days; 74 percent, 3 days; etc.) were plotted on a scatter diagram and an almost perfect correlation was displayed, at a 45-degree angle. The higher the percentage of incomplete data (the X axis), the longer the repair time (Y axis). There seemed no doubt that incomplete information resulted in techs frequently having to make multiple trips to customers' homes, which made it virtually impossible to achieve repairs within two days. The team's scatter diagram is shown in Figure 6.19.

With its root cause analysis verified, the team began the next step: reducing or eliminating that cause.

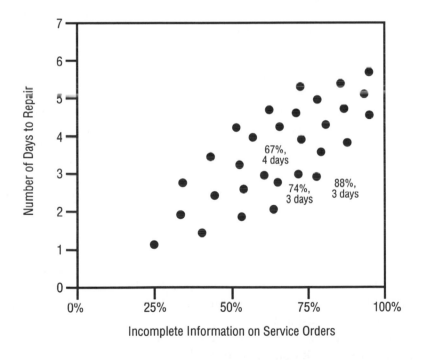

Compiled by:	Ann Jacobson
When:	1/1/94 - 2/28/94

FIGURE 6.19 Relationship Between Late Refrigerator Repairs and Incomplete Information on Service Orders

Step 9: Develop and Test Possible Solutions

Having identified and verified the possible root cause, the Electrons team considered various options to solve the problem once and for all.

Janet referred to the Quality Journey storyboard which contained the "mini-steps" of each of the major ten steps. In Step 9, the process of selecting a solution is related to the PDCA (Plan-Do-Check-Act) cycle.

The team would "plan" and select which solutions to employ to eliminate the root cause of the problem. They would then implement ("do") the selected solution or solutions. In the "check" mode, the team would assess whether the solution(s) were effective (i.e., did they reduce or eliminate the root cause). Finally, they would "act" to change the solution or, if effective, assure that the solution continued to be used (i.e., standardize it).

Before implementing any solutions, the team would make a presentation to the management council to formally communicate the team's Quality Journey and to obtain management approval.

Plan: Selecting Potential Solutions

In the plan stage, the Electrons looked at several different sources of information. Janet urged the team to keep an open mind about possible solutions. They might consider some ideas that could create a breakthrough, or radical improvement, rather than simply speeding up the repair time by 24 hours. One way of thinking, as they gathered information, was based on the concept of "idealized design," or identifying the ideal or perfect situation (i.e., immediate repairs) and working backwards to determine what must be done to arrive at that ideal state (see Chapter 3).

Roberto and Susan interviewed several managers who had been with JAWS for several years, some of whom used to be in the service department. With no ownership in the current process, these managers might have some valuable input.

Jim Peters was a good friend of the owner of Appliance Discounters, a similar store in Cleveland, Ohio. With Jim's approval, Irwin and Ann spent a day with Appliance Discounters' service manager, Wayne Roos. They did an abbreviated form of benchmarking to observe and learn how Appliance Discounters managed to repair refrigerators on the first visit 98 percent of the time.

Chris researched industry trade journals and various electronic publications to learn if there were any innovative solutions which future technology might offer. He readily applied the "idealized design" concept. Chris's approach was that the only ideal solution was instantaneous repair. In his mind, there had to be a way to accomplish it, although he didn't have the foggiest notion how that might happen—yet.

Janet called several refrigerator manufacturers for any input they might provide. The manufacturers might have statistics on what parts were most likely to break, so that JAWS could stock more of those parts.

Tommy spent two hours per day monitoring incoming service calls and interviewing the service order reps. Since they received customers' repair requests, they might have some ideas about how to improve the process. Tommy also spoke to the sales department managers to get their feedback and bounce some ideas off of them.

These activities occupied the team for three weeks. During this period, the team did not meet formally.

At the next meeting, each member gave a brief report. Janet suggested that the team list the various ideas on a flipchart. Some ideas might stimulate new ideas. The list would also lead to a structured evaluation of the ideas.

Over 75 ideas were brainstormed, ranging from using larger trucks (which could carry every conceivable part) to having service techs communicate directly with customers (instead of service reps).

After rehashing these ideas for five hours in an extended meeting, the Electrons multi-voted to reduce the list of 75 ideas to a more manageable number. They agreed on the following nine ideas:

1. Redesign the service form, with a checklist so that the service reps would be more likely to ask the right questions when customers called.

2. Provide special training for the service reps so they would know more about how refrigerators operate, which would allow them to ask more probing questions.

3. Designate certain vehicles for refrigerator repairs so that a full stock of parts would always be accessible.

4. Build slide-in racks for the trucks, with each rack containing a full complement of parts for designated appliances.

5. Equip each vehicle with a cellular phone so that the service tech could speak directly to the customer and attempt to diagnose the

problem over the phone. The tech could avoid an unnecessary trip if the right part was not on the truck.

6. Designate one driver and vehicle, stationed at the service center, for "emergency" deliveries, so that if the tech needed a part, the emergency vehicle could bring it immediately, usually within 30 minutes.

7. Have each tech bring a portable refrigerator which could be left with the customer should a second trip be necessary. This would not eliminate the multiple trips, but it might placate customers who were concerned about spoiled food.

8. Refuse to service certain refrigerator brands which were prone to malfunction. Customers would be referred to factory service centers, even if they had purchased the unit from JAWS.

9. Probably the most unique idea, presented by Chris based on his research, was to install monitoring devices in customers' homes (for a fee, of course), which would monitor refrigerators and other appliances. The monitoring device would not only predict potential failures, but would also identify the cause of a problem when a malfunction occurred. The tech would know exactly what the problem was even before leaving the service center. Chris pointed out that no one else in south Florida employed this system and it would be a great marketing advantage. If this were not an "ideal design," Chris implored, it was the next best thing.

The exhausted team members agreed that they should wait until the next meeting before evaluating the nine possible solutions.

Plan: Selecting a Solution

During the first 20 minutes of the next meeting, Janet reviewed the Quality Journey process the team would use to make its selection. The team would not know for certain whether a solution was effective until it was implemented and the results checked, but it was important to use a structured methodology to choose the proposed solutions.

Janet displayed the solutions selection matrix. On the left-hand side of the three-by-five-foot poster, the team was to list the nine proposed solutions. Each solution would be evaluated and rated by the team according to three criteria: (1) the extent to which the solution was effective and would eliminate the root cause of the problem; (2) whether the solution was practical from the standpoint of cost, the time required to implement it, and how difficult it would be to employ; and (3) the degree to which the solution represented a real value to customers. The poster included a column to represent each of the criteria and a fourth column in which the total of the ratings for each proposed solution could be entered. The fifth column would indicate whether the proposed solution would be analyzed further ("Go"?). The team's matrix is displayed in Figure 6.20.

The criteria for each proposed solution were to be rated on a scale of 1 to 10, the latter being the highest (i.e., best or most effective). When

Potential Solutions	Effective-ness	Practicality (Cost/Time/ Acceptability)	Customer Value	Total	Go/ No Go
1. Redesign Service Form	5	8	6	240	G
2. Training for Service Order Writers	5	5	8	200	G
3. Designate Specialized Trucks	8	3	7	168	
4. Slide-in Racks for Trucks	8	3	7	168	
5. Cellular Phones: Technician Calls Customer	6	5	5	150	
6. Designate Person & Truck for Emergency Deliveries	9	2	4	72	
7. Leave Portable Refrigerator	3	6	5	90	
8. Limit Brands to Repair	9	8	3	216	G
9. Monitoring System	10	2	10	200	Reconsider

FIGURE 6.20   Solutions Selection Matrix: Scale of 1 to 10

all three criteria had been rated for each solution, the ratings would be multiplied. The top score would be 1000 ($10 \times 10 \times 10$). Once the ratings were completed, the two or three solutions with the highest scores would be analyzed further. Janet pointed out that it would be a waste of resources to analyze all nine solutions in detail. The matrix would allow the team to narrow the choices down, based on the best combination of effectiveness, practicality, and customer satisfaction, using their collective experience.

Before beginning the rating process, Janet reminded everyone that the scores should reflect the team's consensus, following ample discussion of logic and facts. In particular, Janet said that the team should not vote or average the ratings. If two people disagreed, there had to be a reason for the difference, which needed to be discussed. Janet pointed to the "Rules of the Road" poster, which called upon everyone to participate and keep an open mind.

Irwin recalled from the training session that it would be less confusing to rate each solution against each of the others, applying one criterion at a time. The nine solutions would be compared to each other from an effectiveness standpoint. The most effective would receive a "10" and the others a lesser rating. Each of the nine would then be rated in terms of practicality and then from a customer value standpoint. The rest of the Electrons agreed that this approach made sense.

Effectiveness

Once the nine potential solutions were entered on the matrix, the team began assessing the effectiveness of each. While Chris's suggestion to install monitoring systems seemed a little bizarre, the team agreed that it was probably the most effective solution since the tech would always know what the problem was, assuming that the monitoring system was functioning properly. Accordingly, the team agreed to rate the suggestion a "10." Janet pointed out that the number itself was not as important as the fact that the other ratings would be in relation to it. The practicality (and cost) of the suggestion would be considered later.

The team agreed that the least effective method would be to loan the customer a portable refrigerator if the tech were unable to complete the repair on the first trip. In addition to not being able to store most customers' food, this solution really did not address the root cause of the problem—that techs did not have the right information when they went on a service call. While Ann and Tommy thought that this solution rated a "1," they finally agreed with the others and reached consensus on a rating of "3."

The Electrons finished the "effectiveness" portion of the matrix in one meeting. If they had any difficulty, it was the tendency to consider the cost of the solution, but Irwin's earlier suggestion kept them focused on the one issue—determining which proposed solution was most effective in dealing with the problem.

Practicality

At the next meeting, the team looked at the practicality of the nine suggestions and considered in general terms whether much cost was involved (cash outlay as well as people's time), how long it would take to implement (days versus months), whether it would be difficult to implement (people issues), and the nuisance factor. Janet stressed that the team was not going to do a detailed cost–benefit analysis at that point; that would occur once the list was reduced to a few solutions. Here the team was just using its experience to ask, in the simplest terminology, whether each idea was practical (i.e., did it make sense?).

Much to Chris's consternation, his monitoring suggestion was deemed not very practical in that it involved a heavy outlay of money for installation, training, monitoring equipment at the service center, and hiring a specialized person to operate the equipment. While the cost might eventually be recovered through subscriber fees to customers, sufficient information was not available to assume that customers would pay for the service. JAWS, as Ann pointed out, was in no position to gamble on such an investment.

Chris was a little upset because he had spent many hours researching the idea. He had taken Janet's suggestion about starting with an "idealized design" literally. Chris even hinted about resigning from the team. Susan whispered loudly to Tommy that worse things could happen. Chris gathered his manual and other materials and prepared to stalk out.

Janet stopped the meeting. She said she was very upset that the team was neglecting the "Rules of the Road" to which they all had agreed in the first meeting. She emphasized that they were a team and were supposed to give everyone's ideas and comments their full consideration, whether or not it impacted their private agendas. Further, Janet exclaimed, none of the team should be making nasty remarks, as Susan had just made. Also, if Susan had something to say, she should have addressed the whole group rather than engaging in side conversations. Susan apologized, and Chris acknowledged that he had probably overreacted to the criticism of his "pet idea." In the back of the room, Joe remained quiet but signaled to Janet that she had done well.

Chris finally admitted that compared to the other suggestions, the monitoring idea was not the most practical. Roberto suggested that the idea be kept on the "back burner" to be revisited if the other ideas were not totally successful. Everyone agreed that the monitoring idea should be rated a "2" in terms of practicality.

At the other extreme, the Electrons readily agreed that redesigning the form and limiting the brands to be repaired would not cost very much and could be implemented easily. Both solutions received an "8" for practicality. The other ratings are shown on the matrix in Figure 6.20.

There was a little time left in the meeting, and Janet suggested that the team postpone the rating of customer value until the following week. She sensed that emotions were running a little high.

After the meeting was adjourned, Janet and Joe held their usual session to critique the meeting. Joe commented on how well the team had been progressing through the matrix, in particular the "effectiveness" column. He was pleased they had decided to rank each column separately to maintain focus. Janet was waiting for the other shoe to drop and asked what she might have done differently to handle the episode between Chris and Susan.

Joe acknowledged his concern but assured Janet that what had occurred was not unusual. Groups go through various stages of development, sometimes being very team oriented, and then revert to more individualistic styles.

In the 1950s, Dr. Bruce Tuckman researched team behaviors and identified five distinct stages: form, storm, norm and perform, and adjourn. So far, the Electrons had engaged in little storming, but today's meeting was just a sample of what can occur. What helps in this situation, Joe tried to say without preaching, is to maintain the team's focus on the problem and the process without losing sight of the basic principles of quality improvement. For example, rather than reach a "standoff" about how practical Chris's idea was, Janet might have encouraged more discussion to allow Chris and others to share their data and facts. If Ann thought the idea was not practical, she should tell the group. If Chris disagreed with Ann, he could present any data he had to support his position.

In general, Joe thought that Janet handled the side remarks well. The only question might relate to timing. She might have asked Chris to stay through the end of the meeting, refocused attention on the meeting agenda, and saved the little lecture for the five-minute end-of-meeting critique portion just before adjourning. Other members might have critiqued Chris and Susan instead, saving Janet from having to do so. Joe thought that the more often a team leader is put in the position of "traffic cop," the more difficult is it to maintain a positive leadership role.

Janet and Joe confirmed their regular session to be held just before next week's Electrons meeting. They would review the agenda and plan for appropriate steps should the Chris and Susan situation recur.

Customer Value

The Electrons assembled again, this time to rate the "customer value" section of the matrix. Tommy reported on his discussions with some of JAWS' sales staff, who were very negative. While limiting brands to repair might make good economic sense, it would result in lost sales. The sales staff viewed JAWS' service department as a competitive advantage.

Roberto acknowledged the point, but expressed concern that what may have been a good selling strategy was backfiring when repairs were not handled well. He asked, "Do we lose potential refrigerator customers by not offering service or lose them later when we aggravate them?"

Janet asked if anyone else cared to comment on the issue. No one spoke up, perhaps in reaction to the previous day's little scuffle. Janet suggested they remain focused on the matrix and whether this proposed solution would increase value to customers compared to the other ideas. Joe nodded his approval.

The discussion picked up and everyone agreed that whether or not the strategy made any sense, customers would not be very satisfied with the policy. Although it might be valuable to JAWS, customers would perceive absolutely no value. Another consideration, probably relating to practicality, was that the policy could not be implemented immediately, because customers who had purchased refrigerators in the past had been told that JAWS would service their products. Not only would customers have to find another place to handle their repairs, but the policy would be directly contrary to what they had been promised when they made their purchases. This idea was rated a "3."

Chris beamed when his monitoring idea was rated by the team as a

"10." Customers would have their repairs made on the first trip, with the bonus of advance warning when a breakdown was imminent.

Some of the other ideas were rated less than "10" because the impact on customer value would not be dramatic. While most of the other ideas might have increased JAWS' efficiency, in the customers' minds, JAWS would just have been performing as expected, nothing more, nothing less. Of all the other ideas, training the service reps to ask more specific questions was rated slightly higher. Customers would be impressed with JAWS' thoroughness and professionalism when the tech arrived to make the repair after the service rep had accurately recorded the problem. Customers became very aggravated when they explained a problem in detail to a service rep over the phone and their comments were summarized as "won't work."

Rankings

With all the ratings completed, Ann multiplied the team's assessment of each of the nine ideas, as reflected on the matrix. The three proposed solutions that received the highest scores were (1) to redesign the service form, (2) to train the service reps, and (3) to limit the brands to be repaired. The matrix reflected the three choices with a "G," to go forward to the next level of analysis.

Chris and Tommy shook their heads. Janet pointed out that this was not the final team decision, but only the basis for deciding which ideas to scrutinize further. The team agreed that since the monitoring idea was a close fourth, it should be reconsidered later. The monitoring idea was in a class by itself, probably the best long-range solution, whereas the other ideas would result in incremental, less dramatic improvements.

Plan: Analyzing the Three Potential Solutions

Janet reviewed the next sequence of steps. First, the team would conduct an in-depth cost–benefit analysis of each solution, followed by a force field analysis, and then prepare an action plan to implement the solution which they decide upon. The team would then make a presentation to the store's management council, which would consist of the service manager, the store manager, and others who had an interest in the outcome. Janet and Joe weren't sure whether the Peters brothers could attend, but Joe knew they would try. Both Jim and Frank were becoming very anxious about the team's progress and authorized the Electrons to meet as often and for as long as possible each week to complete the project.

Cost–Benefit Analysis

The prescribed method in the Quality Journey was to determine the total cost of a problem, including direct and indirect costs (such as rework and extra trips), plus lost revenues which could be attributed.

The next step was to estimate what the cost would be after implementing the proposed solution, which would presumably reflect fewer repeat service calls and related expenses, coupled with the added revenues resulting from increased customer satisfaction. Additional revenues might also be attainable by selling more services (such as service contracts) once the service was reliable.

In effect, the team was to take "before and after" pictures, comparing what the service process was currently costing JAWS to what it would be expected to cost in the future. For example, if the current process cost $350,000 per year and the new process might cost $250,000 per year, the company would "gain" $100,000 a year.

The third step was to determine the cost of implementing the solution, which would reduce the gain. Some solutions would be more expensive than others, depending upon the need for training, equipment purchases, printing, etc. The hypothetical $100,000 gain might quickly disappear if the implementation costs were too high.

As a rule of thumb, Janet said, the cost–benefit analysis should be done over a five-year time frame, considering the benefits for that length of time. Solutions should not be rejected just because they do not pay for themselves overnight. After all, the team was charged with the task of solving problems for the long run rather than coming up with a quick fix. Frank Peters, who attended this meeting, echoed his full support.

Members were divided into three groups so that each of the three proposed solutions would be studied by two team members. There might be some duplication, but the procedure would act as a double-check on each group's data collection and assessment. Each group was to meet with the accounting and sales departments to come up with numbers and estimates.

Tommy wondered why an accountant hadn't been assigned to the team. Joe responded that it was important that the team maintain ownership of the project and that everyone on the team needed to stay involved. Joe's experience was that having "experts" on a team quickly led to members deferring to such experts, which reduced the members' commitment and involvement. Joe reminded the team that the accountants had not been through the training, and while their tracking revenues and expenses may be acceptable for general accounting practices, it was not necessarily suitable for making business decisions, particularly when projections were involved.

The three groups gathered data over the next ten days, interviewing the accountants, store managers, and sales staff. Compiling the actual expenses involved in making repeat trips (and the related loss of service revenue when a tech was unavailable to make other service calls) was not complicated. It was a little more difficult to estimate what a new process might save, because tech and vehicle utilization would increase. It might turn out that JAWS would not need as many techs, unless revenues improved considerably.

What was particularly mind-boggling was having the store managers and sales staff estimate the impact on sales of not changing the process at all (i.e., many repeat trips and customer complaints) and improving the process in one of the three proposed manners. The sales staff was already concerned about the idea of limiting repairs to certain brands. Estimating five years into the future only made matters worse!

Irwin had a novel idea for converting customer dissatisfaction into dollars. In the original Pareto analysis, Irwin noted that there had been few complaints about oven repairs. By comparison, ovens have fewer parts than refrigerators and the tech almost always had the right parts in the truck, requiring virtually no repeat calls.

The team found a high correlation between customer satisfaction with oven repairs and future purchases of JAWS products. Unfortunately, there was also a high correlation between refrigerator repairs and future purchases (or lack of them). About eight out of ten customers would continue to purchase from JAWS if they had a favorable service experience (such as with ovens), compared to only four out of ten who had the opposite experience (such as with refrigerators). The team calculated that for every ten JAWS refrigerator customers, all of whom would eventually need service on their refrigerators, about four would never buy from JAWS again. Another two would probably not buy for other reasons (i.e., moved away). If the satisfaction with refrigerator service equaled the satisfaction with oven service, there presumably would be four additional refrigerator sales for every ten current buyers. But they were currently losing those four potential sales. Revenue losses were projected to be even higher because dissatisfied refrigerator customers presumably would not buy other Jaws' products as well.

Irwin and Susan reviewed the numbers with the sales staff, who agreed that the figures looked right. Frank, who had become the unofficial head of quality at JAWS, hoped the team would not overlook the intangible impact of poor service, which would eventually hurt JAWS' reputation in the community and was directly contrary to one of the company's strategic objectives. Frank recited some of his favorite sayings (e.g., that a dissatisfied customer will tell 40 other people; it's ten times as expensive to get a new customer as to retain an old one).

A cost–benefit analysis was performed on the three proposed solutions. As expected, the least costly proposal to implement was to change the repair policy by limiting home refrigerator repairs to just one brand (General Electric), which had the fewest problems. There would be some lost sales of other brands by not offering repairs, but Susan pointed out that by not creating dissatisfied customers (when the units broke), they might still be able to sell other products (i.e., ovens) to such prospects. Tommy and Ann cringed at this logic, but said they agreed with Susan's revenue estimates.

Redesigning the form would also be very economical to accomplish. Bob and Chris said they could probably do it, with the service reps' assistance, in a week. The only additional expense would be printing the new forms. Instructing the three service reps on the use of the new form was estimated to take about two hours apiece. Based on an estimate that perhaps "only" 3.5 out of 10 refrigerator buyers would never buy from JAWS again, future revenues would improve slightly.

The training proposal would be the most expensive. Each of the three service reps would be given a week of intensive training, including three days devoted to how different refrigerators operate, the critical parts, and what questions to ask when a customer needs a repair. An additional two days would be spent by the reps accompanying techs on service calls to develop a better idea of the problems encountered. Frank liked this idea and commented that this would enhance the reps' credibility with customers, an intangible but important benefit in the long run. The team acknowledged that with turnover running about one in three per year, the training would have to be repeated annually.

After about 20 minutes of discussion, the team agreed with its earlier assessment that reps fielding customers' calls with better questions, coupled with avoiding some repeat trips, would increase customer satisfaction more than the other two solutions. Translating this to reduced dissatisfaction and increased future revenues, the team estimated that the "never buy again" number would be "only" three out of ten, compared to the current four out of ten. They acknowledged that some repeat calls would still occur, but at least the trend would be in the right direction, with relatively little cost. The five-day training was estimated to cost $500 per service rep, including salary and the cost of the tech or service manager's time to do the training. The training would be done on staggered shifts so that the phones would always be covered.

Ann, who had been quiet for the past few meetings, spoke up. She suggested that they combine redesigning the form with providing the intensive training. If customers were going to be asked more questions, the reps needed to have the right document on which to record the information. Combining these ideas might even result in fewer dissatisfied customers and more additional sales than either proposal alone. This was designated Proposal #4 on the matrix. Chris said he was a little shaky about predicting more sales, but agreed with the rest of the group that the "never buy again" category could be reduced to 2.5 out of 10. Thus, implementing both proposed solutions would reduce the "never buy again" category by almost 50 percent! The cost–benefit analysis is shown in Figure 6.21.

Some of the team members seemed uncomfortable with the projections, but Joe assured them that the forecasts were only intended as rough estimates, to be used as a basis for comparing one solution to the others. In fact, lost revenues do not equate directly with profits because of overhead and direct expenses. Also, some expenses may be incurred once while others will be expended each of the five years.

After this exhausting meeting, the team quickly agreed to break until the next meeting, when they would conduct a force field analysis of their selection.

Force Field Analysis

Janet explained that the team needed to identify what might stand in the way of implementing each proposed solution properly (i.e., the restraining forces). Similarly, there might be conditions that would make the solutions workable (driving forces). Some driving forces might offset some restraining forces. The whole purpose was to anticipate difficulties and plan for them (see Chapter 3).

	Current (No changes)	Proposal #1 (Limit brands)	Proposal #2 (Redesign form and minimal training)	Proposal #3 (Extensive training)	Proposal #4 (Combine proposals 2 and 3)
Technician cost (unproductive time)	$65,000	$30,000	$45,000	$20,000	$10,000
Equipment unproductive	5,000	2,500	4,000	2,000	1,000
Service Rep. time lost or duplicated	10,000	7,000	8,000	5,000	4,000
Lost revenues	30,000	45,000	15,000	10,000	5,000
Gross cost	110,000	84,500	72,000	37,000	20,000
Gain/loss from implementing proposal	N/A	25,500	38,000	73,000	90,000
Cost to implement	N/A	1,000	3,000	5,000	8,000
Net gain/loss	N/A	+24,500*	+35,000*	+68,000*	+82,000*
Five year projection	$550,000	+122,500*	+175,000*	+340,000*	+410,000*

*Compared to taking no action

FIGURE 6.21 Cost–Benefit Analysis: One-Year Projection, Except Last Row

Restraining Forces	Driving Forces
Time for training reps on new form	Reduced call-backs
Lack of training space	More sales, referrals
Possible resistance from reps on new form	Top management priority
Wrong diagnosis by reps of problem	Spare office due to retiring manager
Service techs may ignore additional info.	Training of techs, awareness
Budget for training	Less stress on reps
Questionable management commitment, support	Fewer total service calls
Customers might resent extra questions	Manufacturers' training fund
Not enough reps to spend extra time on phone	More time per caller, less rushed
Quota on reps to handle minimum calls per day	
Sales department might resent extra questions to customers	

FIGURE 6.22 Force Field Analysis

At Joe's suggestion, Janet split the Electrons into two groups. Chris, Roberto, and Ann were to brainstorm all the restraining forces on a flipchart, while Susan, Irwin, and Tommy were to brainstorm the driving forces. Their lists for the combined solution are displayed in Figure 6.22.

The biggest restraining force to overcome, which unfortunately did not have a driving force to offset it, was the attitude of the service manager, Hank Bull. It became very apparent that Hank had no great love for customers; to him, they were only necessary evils who were always making unreasonable demands. Hank had previously been service manager at a local stereo store, where customers frequently had to wait three or four weeks to have their amplifiers fixed. In Hank's mind, anybody who wanted any kind of product fixed in two or three days was unreasonable. Even if a repair required five return trips, a refrigerator was usually taken care of within a week. Hank's response to the cost of repeat trips was to raise rates to cover the cost.

It was clear that the ramifications of Hank's attitude would be difficult to counter. His complete cooperation was essential to having the repair form revised and to reinforcing the need for obtaining more information for customers. As it was, Hank chided the service reps if they seemed too "chatty."

Since Hank was monitoring the team's activities closely, questioning their purpose and the time spent in meetings, Janet suggested that the minutes and the force field analysis not refer to Hank directly. They would only indicate that "management commitment" was a restraining force. Hank would probably assume that meant Jim Peters.

Another restraining force, squeezing time for training into the usual hectic pace at JAWS, had no offsetting driving force. However, the lack of training space was offset by the availability of the office of the retiring assistant store manager who was not being replaced.

Action Plan

Problems such as finding the time for training were entered on the action plan (Figure 6.23). Roberto was assigned the task of negotiating with the techs, Hank, and the service reps to schedule the training. Other items were also assigned, even if there were no opposing forces to contend with. It was important that every open item be addressed, with somebody

Date _____

What	Who	When	Indicator of Completion	Completed on Time (Y/N)	Comments
Redesign service order form	Tom and Irwin	10 days from date	Hank, Service Reps, and Techs agree		
Print revised service order form	Ann	30 days from date	Receipt from printer		
Schedule training time for reps	Robert	15 days from date	Memo from Hank, confirming training dates		
Increase awareness of the need to make changes	Janet	20 days from date	Support from management		Probably can't quantify indicator
Reserve training room	Chris	10 days from date	Memo from office manager confirming room		Planning to use former assistant managers office

FIGURE 6.23   Action Plan

assigned to handle it, and a completion date be assigned. Otherwise, something might fall through the cracks.

As noted, "management commitment" was listed as an action item to be addressed. Janet agreed to take responsibility, but the specific action was left nebulous: "to increase awareness." She and Joe decided to deal with "the Hank problem" later.

At this point, the Electrons had examined the problem of late refrigerator repairs and the root causes of the late repairs and decided upon the combined solutions to counter the root causes. Before going further, it was necessary to prepare a presentation for the management council to formally update the council about the team's activities, review the problem-solving efforts, and obtain its approval for the solutions.

Plan: Presentation to Management for Approval

Although the Electrons had kept management up to date on their activities through the distribution of minutes and frequent informal discussions, supplemented by Joe's reports to the management council, it was time for the team to make a formal presentation.

In the presentation of a Quality Journey, the team reviews its data and problem-solving methodology. During the session, team members present for about 20 minutes, and all questions from the council are deferred until the end. While the official reason for the presentation is to secure approval to implement the proposed solutions, it also serves as a form of recognition for the team's efforts. In reality, management has probably approved the solutions informally as it has been kept informed about the team's progress. An ideal presentation should contain no surprises.

Janet and Joe scheduled their presentation for June 15th in the Dade store's training room. Tables were arranged in the shape of a horseshoe, with seating for 15. The team planned to use overheads to illustrate its Quality Journey storyboard process. The four-by-six-foot storyboard was mounted on the wall, next to the projection screen. Janet and Irwin were to make the presentation. Chris, who was uncomfortable making presentations, agreed to handle the overheads. Other team members were responsible for reproducing and distributing copies of the Quality Journey to those in attendance.

The management council included the store manager (Elizabeth O'Douls), the two assistant store managers (Sandra Woodall and Pete Swartz), the service manager (Hank Bull), the regional manager (Sharon

Scott), and the vice president of service for JAWS (Ralph Emerson). Frank Peters also attended. Elizabeth acted as the chairperson for the presentation. A few salespeople and others from the service staff were invited to observe, along with Joe and some of his associates from the VRF Group.

To begin the meeting, Elizabeth announced the purpose and format of the presentation and requested that questions be held until the team's presentation was concluded. Ann distributed copies of the Quality Journey to everyone.

Janet began. She had rehearsed her remarks several times with Joe, but still felt very uneasy. Not only was this her first presentation, but it also was the first presentation of this type at JAWS. She knew Hank Bull was ready to pounce on any gaps in the team's logic or facts, although he might restrain himself in front of Ralph, his boss, and Frank.

Once into the presentation, Janet's words flowed smoothly. She essentially recited what was covered on the overheads, gesturing to illustrate key points. Janet reviewed the Quality Journey through the root cause and verification of the problems (Steps 1 through 8). Irwin then reviewed the nine potential solutions and the team's recommendation to redesign the form and to train the service reps. Both Janet and Irwin related the need to improve in this area to the corporate and departmental balanced scorecards, emphasizing that they would never be in "balance" unless this major source of customer dissatisfaction were eliminated. Altogether, Janet and Irwin consumed 25 minutes, running a little behind schedule.

Elizabeth thanked the team for its presentation and invited all the Electrons to join Janet and Irwin at the front of the room to field questions.

At first, no one had any questions. It appeared that most of the management council was overwhelmed by the amount of analysis that the team had undertaken, something that probably was not apparent earlier. Finally, Elizabeth broke the ice by asking some simple questions, such as how often the team met and for what length of time. Ralph wondered if the idea could be applied at other JAWS' service centers. Others asked what type of difficulties the team may have encountered.

About ten minutes into the questioning, Hank finally raised his hand. Janet thought to herself, "Well, here it comes...."

Hank glanced around the room at Elizabeth, Sandy, Ralph, Sharon, and Frank. He wasn't sure whether he should say what was really on his mind. Finally, he spoke up. "I can't believe what I've just seen. I mean this group put a lot of work into this project, spending over six months just to tell us to change a form, all because a few hysterical idiots want us to drop everything to fix their refrigerators the same day they break! I'll bet you didn't know that the average refrigerator doesn't even break down for at least five years. If you want me to change the damned form and do all this training, I won't get in the way, but I just don't see it!"

Janet and Irwin looked at each other, but before either could say anything, Elizabeth looked over to Hank and asked if his remark was a question. Hank just shook his head in exasperation while doodling on the handout. Frank looked concerned, but didn't say anything except to thank Janet and the rest of the team members for their efforts.

Elizabeth and the management group discussed the team's recommendation for about ten minutes and granted their enthusiastic approval. Hank muttered, "Sure, why not?"

With its presentation completed and approval to proceed obtained, the team was ready to implement its action plan.

Following the meeting, Janet and Joe conferred. Joe expressed his admiration for how well the presentation went, especially since it was a first. Commenting on Hank's little tirade, Joe said it might have solved the "Hank problem," because now there was no doubt as to Hank's attitude toward quality and customer satisfaction. Perhaps further training would cause a shift in Hank's mindset, but Joe thought it unlikely. At this stage, Joe thought that Frank would probably be in touch with him regarding Hank.

That evening, the team went out for a little celebration since an important milestone had been reached. Now all they had to do was make their recommendations work!

Do: Proposed Solutions Implemented

In the first meeting following the successful presentation, the team agreed that redesigning the service form had priority. Once the design was completed, instruction could proceed on how to complete the form.

Ann had contacted the service reps and they agreed to help in the redesign. This ensured their buy-in and virtually guaranteed that the form would be complete and easy to use.

Ann, Bob, and Irwin were scheduled to meet with the service reps the following Friday for preliminary discussions. Ann projected that after two or three meetings with the service reps, drafting the new form could begin. It would then be reviewed by Hank, the reps, and the outside techs.

In the meantime, the other Electrons members began planning for the training sessions.

The draft was revised six times, the last three times because of changes demanded by Hank. In Hank's mind, the proposed questions to ask customers were too detailed. To obtain his approval, the team compromised by enlarging the "other information" block on the form, so that additional data could be entered. Hank thought that too many questions would keep the service reps on the telephone too long, even though the added data might be useful. At long last, the completed draft was delivered to the printer and was promised for delivery by the end of the month.

Even though the team had described the proposed training in its presentation and it was approved by the council, Hank wanted to reopen the issue. He questioned the need for service reps to understand how refrigerators operated and balked at committing more than two days of training, compared to the five days recommended by the team and approved by the management council. Susan learned that Hank was bad-mouthing the Electrons' plan to the service reps and telling them that they could ask customers all the questions they wanted, but their telephone quotas would stay the same!

At the next team meeting, Janet described Hank's roadblocks. Susan asked why they didn't just tell the management council about Hank's sabotage, but since they worked for Hank, that could be risky. Joe sat at the back of the room and stared straight ahead, obviously very concerned.

After the meeting, Joe and Janet remained for a short review of the situation. Joe agreed that the team members would be at risk by approaching Elizabeth, Ralph, or Frank. Joe thought the best way to handle the situation was for Joe to tell Frank himself in their monthly meeting. Frank always wanted to know what was going on and, in particular, why the team might be running behind schedule. Joe could "reluctantly" describe the situation with Hank and let Frank draw his own conclusions.

The newly printed forms were delivered two weeks later. However, no training had been scheduled because of Hank's foot-dragging. The team was reluctant to start using the forms unless they were coupled with the training.

A very demoralized Electrons team sat down at 4:00 p.m. on Friday afternoon to decide where to go from there. Joe arrived a little late, accompanied by Ralph Emerson, Hank's boss. He asked if Ralph could make a statement.

Ralph apologized for infringing on the team's time but thought it was important for them to know that the Dade service center would be under the guidance of a new service manager because Hank had just resigned for personal reasons. After about 30 seconds of stunned silence, Roberto asked about Hank's replacement. Ralph said that the management council was so impressed with Janet's presentation and knowledge of the service process that she was appointed acting service manager, effective immediately. A round of applause filled the room.

After Ralph left, Janet reminded the team members that they needed to begin the training as soon as possible. She said that with the service reps' needs in mind, she would support whatever schedule they might agree upon, just as long as it got started! Joe was grinning from ear to ear.

Later, Joe confided to Janet that he had very little to do with Hank's leaving. Frank had already gotten feedback about Hank's actions and after conferring with Jim had instructed Ralph to remove Hank. Ralph commented that Frank would get no argument for him because Hank's attitude problems flowed in all directions.

The training was completed in three weeks. The next step for the team was to assess whether the new form and the training achieved the results intended: Did complaints decrease? Was the number of repeat trips to repair refrigerators reduced?

Check: Assessment of Results

The team agreed to monitor the results of its solutions for three months, beginning July 1, the same length of time as the initial survey period. Also, three months was long enough to assure that the new measures were really beneficial, after the initial enthusiasm wore off.

During the three months, the team agreed that it would meet about every 30 days to review the data and suggest ways to improve the process even more.

After the three months of data gathering ended, the team prepared new charts, corresponding to the Pareto and other graphs which had been prepared last year. It was important that the formats remain the same, to construct "before" and "after" pictures of the data. Only then could the solutions be evaluated properly.

As might be expected, the first few weeks were a learning experience for the service reps. Previously, their questioning of customers focused on learning the street address and how payment was going to be handled. Now, customers were asked to describe the symptoms of their broken refrigerators, whether there was any cooling at all, whether the refrigerator light was off (suggesting a power problem), whether the freezer was also broken, whether the thermostat was in the right position, etc. It appeared that their increased knowledge of how a refrigerator operates was very useful. Some customers even thought they were speaking with a service tech!

The service reps' morale increased simultaneously, since they felt that their activities served their customers far more than previously. Janet also eliminated the phone quotas, which reduced a great deal of the pressure to complete phone calls in a hurry.

There was a noticeable decrease in grumbling by the techs about having to make repeat trips. Now most of their complaints were about not being kept busy enough since they seemed to have more time on their hands. Janet, now promoted to full-time service manager of the Dade service center, assured them that there would be plenty of work as JAWS' reputation for quality service was on the rise.

More significantly, it appeared that customers were calling less frequently about late repairs, particularly where refrigerators were concerned (see Figure 6.24). Those who did call apparently were surprised by Janet's demeanor, which suggested that Hank had not always been especially helpful or polite.

Janet and the team couldn't wait for the 90 days to end so they could assess the final numbers. Was it their imagination, or were refrigerator repairs taking less time? Because the data fluctuated from week to week, it was difficult to tell. The summary indicators for the balanced scorecard and the key activities were inching in the right direction.

Within a week of the end of the 90-day period, the Electrons compiled the numbers. The Pareto analysis showed that refrigerators no longer constituted the largest percentage of late repairs. VCRs now held that distinction, representing 38 percent of all late repairs. Televisions now amounted to 27 percent, while refrigerators dropped to 23 percent. Other types totaled 12 percent. Chris was concerned that perhaps JAWS might be repairing refrigerators faster, but at the expense of other appliances. Susan acknowledged that Chris's concern might be legitimate except that the total number of late repairs (over two days) had also dropped, from 417 to 194. There were only 45 late refrigerator repairs compared to over 200 previously. The Pareto chart is displayed in Figure 6.24.

Another revelation was that the overall indicator had improved. The

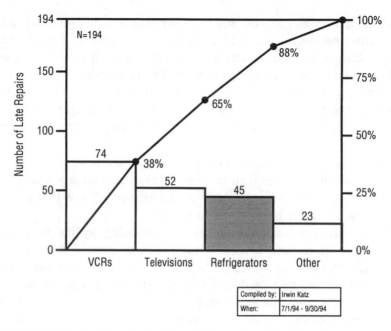

FIGURE 6.24 Late Repairs by Type (More than Two Days)

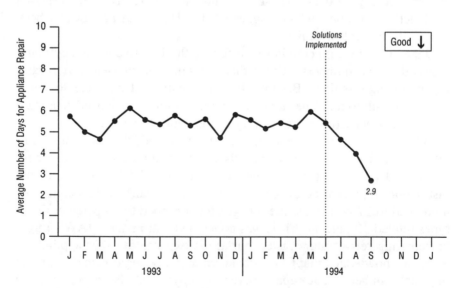

FIGURE 6.25 Average Repair Time (in Days) for All Appliances: JAWS Dade Service Center 1993–1994

average repair time for all appliances was reduced from 4.5 days to 2.9 days. While this did not yet meet customers' expectations for all products, the team was encouraged because it had not yet improved the processes for anything but the refrigerators. It was important to compile the data for all appliances in order to assure that refrigerator repairs were not being expedited at the expense of other products. The changes in the indicator are shown in Figure 6.25.

The Electrons' target for refrigerators was to make the repair in one day. At this point, 19 percent of repaired refrigerators met the target, compared to 7 percent previously. Looking at the two-day numbers, the percentages were 63 and 18 percent, respectively.

Act

Irwin pointed out the obvious—that the numbers were clearly better. The solutions had made a difference. However, the numbers still were not quite good enough. He asked whether the team should just go ahead and make its presentation to the management council or examine some of the other proposed solutions, some of which might require the management council's approval following a presentation.

Roberto thought that more information on the late repairs might be useful. He knew about a few late repairs that had nothing to do with having the right parts (such as when the customer wasn't home), plus another case when the electricity in the neighborhood was off for two days following a bad storm. Not every repair could be made in one day.

It was also possible that if the same process were applied to repairing other appliances, the overall number (2.9 days average) would improve since the team had concentrated only on refrigerators. Janet said that examining the possibility of replicating the process was actually the next step in the Quality Journey, but it would be premature to do so just then.

The team agreed to gather more data on the points Roberto had brought up, so they would not be including those instances when a one-trip repair was not possible. Of the 45 late repairs, 8 could not be done on the first trip because the customer was not home, 2 were due to power outages, and 3 were because of a misunderstanding about JAWS' payment policy (customers were expected to write a check as soon as the repair was completed). Thus, of the 45 late repairs, 11 were for reasons other than insufficient information. Recalculating the repair time for all appliances, the average was reduced from 2.9 to 2.3 days.

Ann suggested that even though some of the delays were technically not part of their problem selection, there had to be some simple solutions to them. Janet said that as service manager, she would handle these herself. She would have the service reps explain the payment policy when customers called in. Techs would call customers just before each service stop to confirm they were home.

Irwin thought the power outages might be dealt with by Jim writing a strong letter to the Florida Public Service Commission, with a copy to the local electric utility's CEO.

The team agreed that some modifications to the form, such as expanding the area for "other comments" and adding a checklist to remind the service reps to cover critical points (confirm date of service, payment policy, etc.), might result in some minor improvements.

Ann volunteered to determine the cost of developing and installing computer screens, which would eliminate the need for forms altogether. She knew a consultant who would do a preliminary estimate for free.

The team agreed that although these changes were not yet ready for implementation, the results were good enough to report to the management council. A meeting was scheduled for the following Thursday.

Second Presentation to Management Council: Results

The Electrons were second on the management council's agenda. Both Jim and Frank Peters attended the meeting. Once again, Janet gave most of the presentation, although Roberto reviewed the results portion of the Quality Journey.

Following the presentation, Frank complimented the team members on their dramatic results. What was incredible, he thought, was that while the service reps were obtaining more information from customers and staying on the phone longer, no additional reps had to be hired! Could it be that they did not have to handle as many complaint calls?

Jim surprised everyone, especially Frank, by displaying overhead transparencies of three letters he had received from customers, thanking JAWS for its very professional approach to ascertaining their refrigerator problems, followed by prompt and reliable repairs. Jim had to admit that he couldn't trace any increased sales to the improved service yet, but it seemed to be a likely result in the near future. The summary measures for the balanced scorecard and the key indicators continued to show marked improvement. Jim thought that it was only a matter of time until the financial portion of the scorecard would begin to improve. Before returning to his seat, he said, "You're certainly making a believer out of me!" Frank and Joe exchanged glances and nodded their approval.

Ralph also expressed his admiration and then asked a blunt question. "How do we move the numbers further? Your target's a good one but we're not there yet. Where do we go from here? How do we repair 100 percent of the refrigerators in one day?"

Irwin spoke for the team. He said that they had instituted two of the proposed solutions and that implementing some of the others would probably result in further improvements. However, the team had concluded that it might not be possible to achieve the target 100 percent of the time without a real breakthrough.

Frank asked what Irwin meant. Irwin placed the solutions selection matrix on the overhead projector and pointed to the ninth solution, the monitoring idea. He described how it would operate, the advantages, and the projected cost. "This," Irwin stated emphatically, "is the only way we're going to make this process foolproof! Everything else we do is just tinkering, making gradual improvements. Just think, we can use this idea for all appliances, not just refrigerators. It will also be a new revenue stream for us, besides giving us a competitive advantage! Ralph, Frank, you want 100 percent? This is the only way we know of, short of using helicopters to fly customers' refrigerators directly to our service center!"

"I think we get the message," Jim interjected. "Let's look over those numbers again and give it some serious thought. I'll bet that introducing a new service before our competitors can react would also improve our rating on the innovation part of the scorecard. In the meantime, didn't you say that we could begin making more improvements just by doing the same thing for all appliances and using your ideas in other locations?"

Janet remarked that the team had already begun thinking about replicating the new process for other types of appliances, the next step in the Quality Journey. She said the team hoped to present its Quality Journey to the other JAWS service centers.

Ralph said that as far as other centers were concerned, the sooner they began using the new process the better! In his mind, whether they used it was not an option on their part!

Elizabeth thanked the team for its presentation and said she looked forward to hearing how the replication proceeded. Jim restated his intention to examine the monitoring idea and said that he would meet with the management council when he had all the information. He reminded everyone that it would be many months before the monitoring idea could be implemented, so the replication efforts needed to proceed. Not only would the monitoring equipment have to be selected and installed, but enough customers would have to be persuaded to subscribe in order to make it truly effective.

Frank and Joe invited the team members to dinner at The Rusty Pelican on Key Biscayne as a way of celebrating their accomplishments to date. The team's work was far from done. Replication was not as easy as it sounded.

Step 10: Standardize the Process

At the next team meeting, Janet again thanked the team members for their help in making the presentation. While Janet and Roberto made the actual presentation, the others had helped prepare the overheads and handouts and participated in the rehearsals.

The next item on the agenda was to standardize the new process for handling refrigerator repairs. By documenting and describing the process, the team could be virtually certain that its efforts would continue to pay dividends. From their training, the team members knew that improvements were often short-lived without a process to assure standardization. Once the process was standardized and a Quality Journey control system was in place, the team could consider replication.

The standardization process began with revising the process flow diagram, or flowchart, to accurately describe the new process. In Step 4, a flowchart was developed to show the existing process. A few other changes were also incorporated, such as assuring the availability of a tech prior to scheduling an appointment (previously, customers would have to be called back if no one was available to make the repair). The revised flowchart is presented in Figure 6.26.

Through the Quality Journey control system, the measuring points were designated, the formulas for calculating the measurements were noted, and the appropriate persons were designated to make the ongoing measurements.

Once the flowchart was revised, the team completed the rest of the

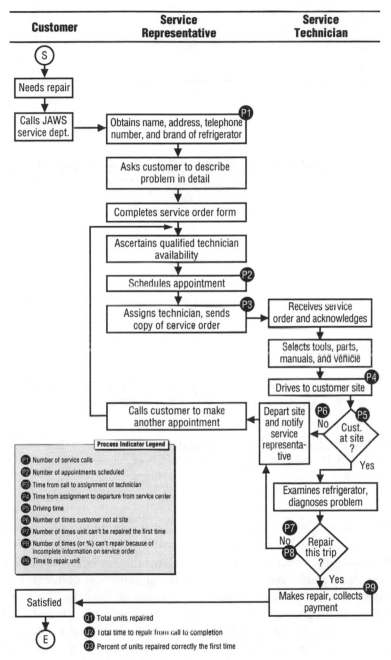

FIGURE 6.26 Micro-Level Flowchart: Dade County Service Department (Process Description of Service Calls for Customer-Site Refrigerator Repair, Including Process (P) and Quality (Q) Indicators)

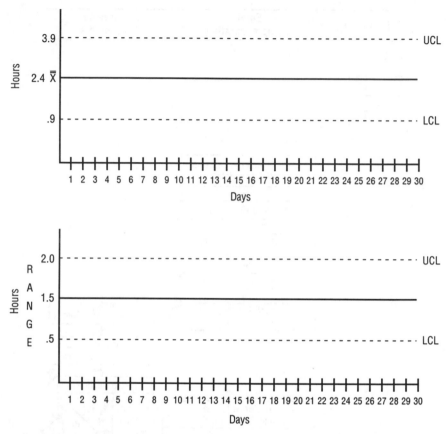

FIGURE 6.27   x̄,R Control Chart to Monitor Time Between Customer Calls to JAWS and Technician Departure to Customer Site (Based on Sample of Five per Day)

control system. Control charts (see Chapter 3) are employed after sufficient data (usually 30 data points) are collected. By tracking data on a control chart, the process owners will know whether or not their process has remained stable and predictable (i.e., in statistical control). One of the control charts to be employed is displayed in Figure 6.27. This particular chart would be used to track the average time (based on five samples per day) between customer calls and techs departing the service center to make the repairs. Other charts would track the average drive time, time at customers' premises, and percentage of complete forms.

Because Ann had just completed VRF's process management course which covered these topics, she volunteered to prepare the first draft of the control system. Chris offered to help in the data collection and analysis to be used in constructing the control charts.

Ann and Chris presented their Quality Journey control system to the rest of the Electrons two weeks later. One key indicator was the amount of information collected on the form compared to the number of applicable data blocks. Depending upon the type of problem, the number of questions to ask customers could range from 3 to 14.

Prior to the team meeting, Susan and Chris reviewed the control system with the service reps to verify that the flowchart accurately depicted the new process. Actually, the reps had already improved upon the process by putting the service center computer on the JAWS network. This enabled them to know instantly which model refrigerator a caller owned. They also planned to create a new file to track service work for each customer, thus maintaining a permanent "life history" of each appliance a customer owned. They thought it might be useful to sell preventative maintenance contracts and to send reminders to customers that their units should be inspected.

The team marveled at Ann and Chris's control system and formally adopted it for the Quality Journey. Janet said that not only would the control system assure that the process would continue to be used, but it would also be instrumental in the replication process, in addition to being a training tool for new employees.

Standardization: Replication—Other Appliances

With the Quality Journey control system finished, Janet said that the team needed to create similar systems for other appliances which were serviced in the home. This included stoves, microwave ovens, dishwashers, washers and dryers, water heaters, air-conditioning units, satellite dishes, and large-screen televisions. While the approach was to be the same as for refrigerators (i.e., asking better questions when a customer calls), the questions would have to relate to each specific type of appliance. Also, because it seemed very helpful for the service reps to know something about how the appliances functioned, some training would need to be scheduled.

Each team member agreed to work on one or more types of appliances to develop a specialized service order form, incorporating input from the service reps and repair technicians. Fortunately, some appliances, such as clothes dryers, were simpler to operate than refrigerators.

Drafts of the new forms were ready within three weeks. With minor changes, all were approved and sent to the printer the next week. Two weeks later, JAWS would begin using the new process for all appliances!

This also permitted the training to be completed by the time the forms arrived from the printer. The training ranged from two to six hours, depending upon the appliance. As an interim measure, so as not to overwhelm the reps, each rep was trained on only three types of appliances.

Janet announced to the team that the first stage of replication had been completed.

Standardization: Replication—Other Locations

Although Ralph Emerson, vice president of service, plus Jim and Frank Peters were solidly behind applying the Electrons' new process at other service centers, there was a lot more involved than simply copying and distributing the Quality Journey.

This became evident at the first presentation at the Broward (Ft. Lauderdale) center. The techs and service reps politely listened to Roberto's presentation, but asked no questions. Ralph was determined to learn their reaction and probed further. He probably wished he hadn't. The Broward group didn't think their customers were bothered by repeat trips because there had not been many complaints. Also, Broward was different from Dade County and had different conditions, or so they said. It also appeared that the next logical step was to eliminate some of the techs' jobs. Why should they shoot themselves in the foot?

Following the presentation, an exasperated Ralph sat down with George Mills, the Broward service manager. George was more than willing to try the Electrons' approach, but admitted that he would have a tough time getting everyone's cooperation. George reminded Ralph that it wasn't like the old days when he could fire anyone who wore the wrong color shirt. George said his influence had even decreased since the Peters brothers had implemented all these new programs, including "all that empowerment stuff." He had been through some of the training and it made sense to him, but hardly anybody else knew much about the program, although they knew just enough to sabotage his attempts at management.

George agreed to think of ways to generate more enthusiasm among the Broward service staff. Ralph acknowledged that ramming the new process down their throats would be worse than doing nothing. Perhaps Broward would prove to be the exception.

The following week, Ann made a presentation at the Orlando (Orange County) service center. The techs and reps weren't so polite. They interrupted her often and called the approach ridiculous. The general attitude was that the Orlando center was doing just fine and that it didn't need a bunch of people from Miami telling them how to do their jobs. Ralph's meeting with James Brown, the service manager at Orlando, didn't fare any better than the meeting in Broward.

Ralph canceled the rest of the presentations scheduled for the month and suggested a meeting with Jim and Frank, plus Janet and Joe.

They all agreed that their replication plans may have been naive. It would be hard to expect the Broward or Orlando staffs to have any buy-in or much sense of ownership. Maybe the Electrons should have kept the other service centers informed while they were progressing through the Quality Journey, even inviting their input. Also, they admitted that they had not tuned into the staffs' favorite radio station, WII-FM, or "What's in it for me?" Why should anyone on those staffs want to do things differently? If anything, it sounded as if they might lose their jobs if efficiency improved.

Frank was really dismayed over a fundamental issue. The real power of having a team solve a problem is the ability to reproduce the solution in other places, but how do you do that without stepping on toes? Everybody looked to Joe for the answers. Perhaps Joe had run into this situation with other clients.

"I see several underlying issues here," Joe began. "First of all, you have the natural human tendency to resent somebody else telling you how to do your work, even if they happen to be right. Second, it sounds as if the Broward and Orlando people don't see any need to change, or they're not sure how the change is related to solving any problems they may have. Surely, they must get some complaints! Also, maybe they resent the Electrons team. All the service people at JAWS went through the training together but only the Electrons have made any real progress. The Orlando team spent six months trying to decide which brand of screwdriver works best, and then they disbanded the team. Finally, you've got the security issue. Many people associate Florida Power & Light's layoffs with its winning a big quality prize. High quality means fewer jobs in some people's eyes!"

"That's a pretty good summary," Jim remarked, "but how are we going to deal with this thing? Just let everybody solve their own problems and keep the solutions to themselves? Our old military style of leadership, as you called it, doesn't sound so bad now! At least I didn't have to worry about hurting people's feeling when I told them to do something! And to think we've invested all this time and money..." Frank was sinking lower in his seat.

Joe was getting a little red in the face. He responded: "Jim, you hired me to help you through this transition. You remember we cautioned at our first meeting that changing cultures and management style would not be a piece of cake. I strongly recommended that we engage full-time facilitators for all your teams, but you vetoed the idea. Let me give you another recommendation, one I was going to suggest next month."

"Joe, anything you have on your mind, please say it," a pained Frank said quietly.

"OK. This has worked for some companies. I didn't think we were quite there yet, but the idea is to have an annual Chairperson's Cup coupled with a service exposition or Expo. The concept is to have selected service staff, including all team leaders, facilitators, and service managers, attend a day-long series of presentations by ten teams which we have identified as having the best Quality Journeys. The next day would be devoted to having Expos, with display booths set up for all teams to display and talk about their Quality Journeys.

"Also, every three months, team leaders and facilitators would meet at Quality Forums, or retreats, to discuss quality issues and share any progress they have made. At all of these events, both you and Frank should participate to show your support and to add to the recognition."

Jim was growing a little impatient. After thanking Joe for what seemed like "a nice idea," he tried to get him to explain how it would help solve their current problem. Ralph and Frank also failed to see the connection.

"Everything I just said doesn't directly help our current problem, but there is some relationship. Teams put out a lot of effort in solving problems. Just ask Janet. The Chairperson's Cup and the Expos are a way to recognize those efforts. The recognition comes in two doses, one from management and the other from peers.

"Coupled with the quarterly meetings, a lot of good information will be shared and publicized. As the meetings occur and teams tell others what they're working on, you'll find that groups like Broward or Orlando will be asking for details about how problems were solved. They'll be begging teams like the Electrons to make presentations. It's really just simple psychology, letting the idea to replicate come from the other service centers.

"Another idea is to put your Quality Journeys on the computer network, linked to a database. When a team is assigned or selects a problem, the first thing it should do is check whether another team has already solved the same problem. If so, then they would contact the other team for more information. Instead of feeling resentment from being told how to do something, they may be grateful for saving them some time.

"Publish a newsletter that talks about results. Whet people's appetite for more information! Even if the service department thinks it can live with a certain level of customer headaches, store managers may have a different perspective. Their bonuses now depend on customer satisfaction, don't they?

"Yes, it probably was wishful thinking that we could stand there and tell other service centers about our great new process in Dade and expect them to do handstands. In retrospect, it would have been better to have publicized the Electrons' efforts and the improvements in productivity and customer satisfaction. Perhaps the store or service managers at Broward and Orlando would have wanted to achieve the same results in order to meet their financial objectives. Maybe they would have contacted Janet for more details and requested a presentation. The approach makes all the difference in the world!

"Jim and Frank, in my opinion, you need to do two more things. I'll tell you and then I'll shut up. When a Quality Journey is considered for replication, other areas have got to be free to modify it for their own circumstances. I understand that the biggest concern among Broward customers is not refrigerators, but air conditioners. Who knows, maybe they will study the Electrons' process and find a way to improve it.

"The other thing is, and I know this may sting, but I think it is essential that you go on record that no one will ever lose their job at JAWS because of the quality initiative. There's just too much skepticism among the employees that they're working themselves out of jobs. And, Jim and Frank, if you're really committed to your quality plan, and truly believe in it, you should expect to be hiring, not firing, people. I don't see how such a promise could hurt you. Enough said."

No one said anything for a few minutes. Frank finally broke the silence by clarifying his understanding that Joe was recommending that the Electrons make no more presentations unless requested to do so. Joe said that was correct, but reiterated his point that there had to be some method of publicizing the Electrons' efforts.

Jim reluctantly went along and asked Frank to develop some of the publicity and recognition ideas Joe had suggested.

As it turned out, Joe was right on target. Within three months of publication of the first "Quality Newsletter," in which the story of the Electrons' Quality Journey was featured, the new process, with minor modifications, was in place at all but two of the JAWS service centers.

Janet was pleased to report that the replication at other locations had virtually been completed and that the team could proceed to the end of its Quality Journey. While it was not an official step, it was an important one nonetheless.

Self-Assessment and Future Activities

Janet reviewed the last step with the team. She said that the team needed to PDCA its own activities (i.e., what lessons did they learn that would benefit their future Quality Journeys). Next they needed to consider what, if anything, should be done regarding the new process.

Janet asked each team member to state something that the team did very well and something that might be done differently the next time.

The list summarizing the things that went well included:

- After the earlier blow-up involving Chris, the team began to function more like a team and everybody was more at ease and willing to listen to others' ideas.

- The team members frequently volunteered to do assignments, with everybody sharing.

- Used service reps' input and adopted it when feasible, assuring their buy-in.

- Very customer focused.

- Followed Quality Journey process well and didn't get off track.

- Employed data well. Really made a big difference.

- Support from Jim, Frank, and Joe was crucial.

The list of things that could be improved included:

- Attendance at meetings was high (97 percent), but two members always had to be reminded that the meetings were starting. They should attend without prompting.

- Meetings frequently ran over the allotted time.

- Perhaps Hank should have been kept better informed early on.

- Replication among other service centers should be handled differently.

- Janet should not have done all the management council presentations.

Regarding future activities, the team agreed that for the next six months it would monitor the results of replicating the new process to other appliances and at the other locations.

The team agreed that Janet would be the team's liaison to Jim regarding the monitoring system. As he had promised, Jim Peters had researched the cost of the system. A survey of customers was currently underway to learn if they would pay a monthly subscription fee and whether they perceived a benefit.

Final Presentation to Management Council

The very last event was the team's presentation of its entire Quality Journey to the management council. The meeting was attended by both Jim and Frank.

Chris and Ann handled the presentation. Once again, in addition to describing their Quality Journey, the Electrons' presentation linked their results to improvements in the broader picture, the balanced scorecard, and measurement of key activities. Questions were very limited, as the presentation was largely a vehicle for recognition.

Chris stated that the Electrons had been selected as one of the top ten teams to make a presentation at the first Chairperson's Cup the following month.

Following the presentation, Jim and Frank Peters took the team members and Joe to lunch at Jim's private club in Coconut Grove. Each member was presented with an acrylic paperweight inscribed with his or her name, with the JAWS quality logo etched around it.

On behalf of the Electrons, Janet thanked Jim and Frank and promised to surprise them about their next Quality Journey.

BIBLIOGRAPHY

Ackoff, Russell L., "Toward a System of Systems Concepts," *Management Science,* Vol. 3, No. 11, 1971.

_____ , *Redesigning the Future,* New York: Wiley, 1974.

_____ , "Does Quality of Life Have to Be Quantified?" *General Systems,* Vol. XX, 1975.

_____ , *The Art of Problem Solving,* New York: Wiley, 1978.

_____ , *Creating the Corporate Future,* New York: Wiley, 1981.

_____ , *The Democratic Corporation,* Oxford: The Oxford University Press, 1994.

Ackoff, Russell L. and Emery, Fred, *On Purposeful Systems,* New York: Aldine Atherton, 1972.

Ackoff, Russell L. and Vergara, Elsa, "Creativity in Problem Solving and Planning: A Review," *European Journal of Operations Research,* Vol. 7, p. 4, 1981.

Adams, James, *Conceptual Blockbusting,* San Francisco: W.H. Freeman, 1974.

Andersen, Barry, *The Complete Thinker,* Englewood Cliffs, NJ: Prentice-Hall, 1980.

Chems, Albert and Davis, Louis, *The Quality of Working Life,* Vols. 1 and 2, London: Collier Macmillan, 1975.

Churchman, West, *The Systems Approach,* New York: Delacorte Press, 1968.

Cutterbuck, David, "The Future of Work," *International Management,* August 1979.

DeBono, Edward, *Lateral Thinking for Management,* England: American Manufacturing Association, 1971.

Dickson, John, *Systems Thinking,* Harmondsworth, England: Penguin Books, 1969.

_____ , "The Plight of Middle Management," *Management Today,* December 1977.

Durmaine, Brian, "Why Do We Work?" *Fortune,* December 26, 1994.

Elliot, Roland, "The Challenge of Managing Change," *Personnel Journal,* March 1990.

Emery, Fred, "Participative Design: Effective, Flexible, and Successful, Now!" *Journal for Quality and Participation,* January/February 1995.

Emery, Fred and Thorsrud, Einar, *Democracy at Work,* Leiden: Martinus Nijhoff Social Sciences Division, 1976.

Emery, Merelyn, *Searching for New Directions in New Ways for New Times,* Canberra: Ontario Quality of Work Life Center, 1982.

Ewing, D., "Discover Your Problem-Solving Style," *Psychology Today,* December 1977.

Fenwick, P. and Lawler, E., "What You Really Want from Your Job, *Psychology Today,* May 1978.

George, Claude, *The History of Management Thought,* Englewood Cliffs, NJ: Prentice-Hall, 1968.

Gharajedaghi, Jamshid, "On the Nature of Development," *Human Systems Management,* Vol. 4, 1984.

Guiliano, Vincent, "The Mechanization of Office Work," *Scientific American,* September 1982.

Gunn, Thomas, "The Mechanization of Design and Manufacturing," *Scientific American,* September 1982.

Hackman, J. Richard and Suttle, J. Lloyd, *Improving Life at Work,* Santa Monica, CA: Goodyear Publishing, 1977.

Hayes, John, *The Complete Problem Solver,* Philadelphia: Franklin Institute Press, 1981.

Jackson, K. F., *The Art of Solving Problems,* New York: St. Martin's Press, 1975.

Kaplan, R. S. and Norton, D. P., "The Balanced Scorecard—Measures That Drive Performance," *Harvard Business Review,* January–February 1992.

Koberg, Daniel and Bagnall, Jim, *The Universal Traveler: A Soft Systems Guide to Creativity, Problem Solving, and the Process of Reaching Goals,* Los Altos, CA: William Kauffman, 1974.

Main, Jeremy, *Quality Wars,* New York: The Free Press, 1994.

Maslow, Abraham, *Motivation and Personality,* New York: Harper and Row, 1954.

Newell, A. and Simon, H., *Human Problem Solving,* Englewood Cliffs, NJ: Prentice-Hall, 1972.

Ouchi, William, *Theory Z: How American Business Can Meet the Japanese Challenge,* Reading, MA: Addison-Wesley, 1981.

Roth, William, "Comparing the Effects of Cooperation, Competition, and Conflict on the Speed with Which Different Personality Types and Personality Type Pairs Can Generate Useful Solutions to Problem," Dissertation, University of Pennsylvania, 1982.

————, "Get Training Out of the Classroom," *Quality Progress,* May 1989.

————, "Try Some Quality Progress Glue," *Journal for Quality and Participation,* December 1989.

————, *Work and Rewards: Redefining Our Worklife Reality,* New York: Praeger, 1989.

————, *A Systems Approach to Quality Improvement,* New York: Praeger, 1991.

————, "The Dangerous Ploy of Downsizing," *Business Forum,* Los Angeles: California State University, Fall 1993.

————, *The Evolution of Management Theory: Past, Present, Future,* Delray Beach, FL: St. Lucie Press, 1993.

Roth, William and Ferguson, Douglas, "How to Play the Teambuilding Game," *Pulp and Paper International,* August 1991.

Rubach, Laura, "Downsizing: How Quality Is Affected as Companies Shrink," *Quality Progress,* April 1995.

Ryder, J. A. Jr., "Improving and Measuring Corporate Performance with the Balanced Scorecard," unpublished.

Schon, Donald, *Beyond the Stable State,* London: Temple Smith, 1971.

Stayer, Ralph, "How I Learned to Let My Workers Lead," *Harvard Business Review,* November–December 1990.

Strategic Management in Corrections Tool Workbook, Management and Behavioral Science Center, The Wharton School, University of Pennsylvania, May 1980.

Taylor, Frederick, *The Principles of Scientific Management,* New York: Harper, 1911.

Townsend, Patrick and Gebhardt, Joan, "Measurement: Neither a Religion nor a Weapon," *TQO,* October 1992.

Trist, Eric, "The Evolution of Socio-Technical Systems," *Issues in the Quality of Working Life,* No. 2, Ontario: Ontario Ministry of Labor, 1980.

Trist, Eric, Higgins, G. W., Murray, H., and Pollock, A. B., *Organizational Choice,* London: Tavistock Publications, 1963.

Von Bertalanffy, Ludwig, "General Systems Theory: A Critical Review," *General Systems,* Vol. VII, 1962.

Wilkerson, James L., "Merit Pay Reviews: They Just Don't Work!" *Management Accounting,* June 1995.

INDEX